kids' crafternoon
papercraft

kids' crafternoon
papercraft

25 projects for a crafty afternoon

edited by Kathreen Ricketson

hardie grant books
MELBOURNE · LONDON

Contents

Introduction

Making stuff and getting crafty is fun! While you experiment, create and make stuff with your hands and your imagination, you are teaching yourself new skills like project planning and decision-making. You are also expressing your creativity, emotions and ideas. So when your parents tell you to stop mucking about and do your homework, you can tell them that what you are doing may look like fun but it is actually work! In fact, you should encourage your parents to get creative with you as it may just help them to relax too. So put on your favourite music, grab a plate of chocolate chip bikkies and get cracking!

Use your imagination

By using your imagination and a few simple materials you have on hand, you can make something cool. Grab a pile of paper and spend the afternoon making paper aeroplanes, then test them out in the backyard. Rummage in the recycling bin for some cereal boxes and make a super-cute monster piñata that's too adorable to smash open. Whip up some origami cubes, which you can hang on a string of LED lights in your room, then fill the leftovers with water to lob at your brothers and sisters. You might feel inspired to make some owl cards for someone special or make a paper pet to keep you company in your room. So many projects – so little time. All the projects in this book are easy to change to suit yourself, so if you like a concept, but want to test out your own designs, or use materials from your recycling box, go for it!

Get crafty

If you are new to papercrafts, and you haven't used a craft knife before, don't fret at all. This book will take you through the basics and show you some super-fun projects to get you started. Nothing is too difficult: some projects might take a bit of extra time and patience, but you will succeed.

If you are already a fairly confident crafter then you can get stuck straight into all the projects in this book. Whatever your skill level you will find something to make. Take your time to read through the instructions and gather your supplies before starting. And remember to stay calm, take plenty of refreshment breaks and ask for help if you need to. And don't get stressed: your crafts don't have to be perfect. The most important thing is that you made it yourself and had fun doing it!

Tools & Materials

You can find lots of different kinds of paper just by searching around your house or heading out to the local craft or stationary store. You don't need special tools or fancy equipment for most of the projects in this book – you will probably find everything you need right at home.

PAPER

Recycled papers. Collect giftwrapping paper, brown paper bags, coloured envelopes and cards with cool designs. Cereal and shoe boxes come in handy; magazines and newspapers are good to have on hand. You can even save paint colour cards that you can get for free from the hardware store. You can also save interesting road maps, comic book pages, sheet music, postcards, stamps and stickers – it's all good stuff.

Basic supplies. You will probably use regular A4 copy paper, tissue paper and paper napkins in different colours that you can get from the newsagent or stationery store – even the local corner shop will probably have them in stock.

Specialty papers. Some designs call for origami paper. This paper comes in different colours, patterns and sizes: it is square, and can be found in craft stores. You may also need double-sided, heavy-weight paper, card stock, or scrapbooking paper. These can also be found in craft stores, newsagents or specialty papercraft shops.

EXTRAS

Pop dots and Velcro dots are fun extras that you can use to make 3D cards or attach items to other items. You'll use these when making the Owl Cards on page 124 and the Shadow Box on page 74. You can get these from craft stores, or substitute thick cardboard with double-sided tape.

Brads or split pins are pins with a split end, and the top is often decorative. You push the pin through a small hole and split the two points, pressing them against the back of the paper or card to hold the brad in place. They are generally used to join two pieces of card where movement is required: you'll use these in the Articulated Puppet projects on page 28.

Embellishments are any materials that, while not essential to the project, can jazz it up a bit: rubber stamps, paper scraps, beads, embroidery thread, stickers, postage stamps, glitter glue, mini pompoms, ribbons and buttons. Keep a box with a collection of all your bits and pieces.

Freezer paper and iron-on interfacing are specialty materials that can be found at craft or sewing stores. Freezer paper comes in a roll and is great for making stencils. One side is smooth and waxy and the other is slightly rough. You trace your design onto the rough side, and the waxy side is then ironed with a hot iron onto the surface of the paper or fabric: it sticks temporarily and can be easily peeled away. You'll need some of this to make the Under-the-Sea Stencils on page 62. Iron-on interfacing is a bit like stiff fabric; you iron it onto the wrong side of your material and it adheres permanently. It adds stiffness to your material that you might need in some projects. This will come in handy for the Pet Menagerie project on page 36.

PROTECTIVE MATERIALS

You will need **sheets of newspaper** to protect your work surface when painting, gluing or doing any messy work.

Thick cardboard that you can recycle from cardboard boxes is necessary to lay out under your project if you are doing any hole punching. This sort of heavy cardboard also works reasonably well as a substitute if you don't have a proper cutting mat.

A plastic apron, old work shirt or other **clothing protector** is good to have on hand when doing messy work too.

TOOLS

Many of the tools that you will need can be found around your house. Gather up these items and keep them stored in a shoe box in your craft supply area, that way you won't have to hunt them down each time you want to make something.

String, twine, and twist ties. Salvage these from packaging and keep them in a zip-lock bag.

Sticky things. Masking tape, double-sided tape, glue sticks and PVA glue are all essential items to have in your craft supplies and you can probably pick these up at the local shops if you don't already have them.

Paper scissors. These are essential, and you might like to have a larger pair and a small pair for different uses. You can get a set of these pretty cheaply at your local shops.

Paints. Acrylic paints, glitter paints, paintbrushes, foam paint rollers and old plastic trays are essential: collect different paint colours gradually, but start off with tubes of white, black, blue, red and yellow and you can mix any colour you want.

Ice-block sticks, barbecue skewers, chopsticks, bits of dowel, binder clips and thin wire. All of these are useful. You can pick up thin wire from beading, craft or hardware stores. Ice-block sticks and barbecue skewers are likely to be found in your kitchen drawer – if not, you can get them from the local supermarket or hardware store.

SPECIALTY TOOLS

Some tools you may not have readily available and you might have to take a trip to the local craft store to find them. You won't need these for many of the projects and most of them are not essential, but they make your life easier and add a little extra charm to your finished work. Save up your money and collect these gradually over time.

Awl and bone folder. These are specialty book-binding tools that can be found in a craft store. An awl is basically a sharp, heavy needle with a handle that is used to punch fine holes into thick paper, card or through many layers of paper at once. You can substitute a heavy darning needle or small craft hole punch (or even a nail will do the trick). A scoring knife or bone folder is used to score your paper: scoring creates a line or depression in heavier card that will help you make an even crease when you fold. You can substitute a butter knife. You will also need a ruler.

Craft punches. These come in all sizes and shapes and are a fun, if not essential, addition to your craft supply box. If you are planning on adding a couple to your collection, start with some basic circle cutters as you will be likely to use these a lot. A small hole punch is also really handy.

Cutting knife, steel ruler and cutting mat. These three items go hand in hand. While many of the projects in this book use scissors, there are some projects where there is simply no substitute for a craft knife. So if you are planning on using one, make sure you have a cutting mat, which will protect your table (a piece of thick cardboard works too) and a strong ruler.

Sewing machine. There are a couple of sewn paper projects in this book that require the use of a sewing machine, so if you have access to one you are lucky. You won't need to be an expert sewer, you will only need to know how to sew a straight line, so first ask if you can use the sewing machine and then practise on some scrap paper. Sewing on paper will blunt the sewing needle, though, so check if there is a spare needle you can use and keep this aside for your paper-sewing needs. If you don't have access to a sewing machine, you can hand sew the couple of projects in this book: it may take a little longer but may even look nicer in the end. When hand sewing on paper you will need a strong sewing needle – a darning or embroidery needle will do – and some strong thread such as linen or embroidery thread. You will be doing only the simplest of stitches – a simple running stitch. See the techniques section below for a 'how-to'.

Pinking shears and decorative paper-edging scissors. These types of scissors have various pretty shapes you can use to create decorative trims on cards.

Basic Techniques

SEWING

Using fusible interfacing. Fusible interfacing can be found in any craft or fabric shop. When adhered to your paper, it will make it stronger and less likely to tear. There are different thicknesses of fusible interfacing that are suitable for various projects, and they have either single- or double-sided tape. For projects in this book you will need a medium-weight, single-sided, fusible adhesive. If you're unsure about the type to buy, ask for help.

The interfacing makes a permanent bond, therefore it is important to get it right the first time – since after you've set the fusible interfacing, there's no undoing it. You might want to test a scrap on your paper first before doing the whole piece. Be sure to read the manufacturer's directions before starting.

1. Place your paper on your ironing board, wrong side up. Centre your interfacing on top of it, adhesive side down (the adhesive side is slightly rough).
2. Set your iron to medium heat with the steam setting on.
3. Press your hot iron onto your interfacing, using downward pressure for about 15 seconds. When moving your iron to another section, lift and press rather than sliding your iron. Leave the interfacing to cool for a minute before checking if it has adhered; if it has not, repeat this process.
4. Leave your paper in place until it has cooled completely and then use it for your project.

Hand sewing. To sew into paper use an embroidery needle and thread – rather than a regular sewing needle and thread – as this will be stronger. If you are having trouble pushing the needle into the paper, you might like to first make holes in the paper using an awl, a larger embroidery needle or even a small nail. Press the awl or nail into the paper where you need to stitch at 1 cm intervals. Use a piece of heavy cardboard or foam to protect your work surface.

Running stitch can be used for creating decorative lines and as a practical stitch for hemming or joining two pieces of material together. Sewing onto paper can make your projects look really stylish. Try sewing designs onto cards, borders on letters, or even sewing your illustrations onto paper and framing them.

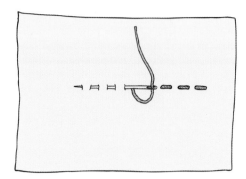

Running stitch is really easy. Just pass the needle in and out of the paper, trying to keep the same length in the stitch and the space between stitches.

Adding buttons to your projects is a really cute way of embellishing them: you can sew buttons onto cards, handmade books and onto the Pet Menagerie on page 36. If you want to get fancy with your buttons you could choose two buttons that lie on top of each other nicely and attach them at the same time.

1. First mark with pencil where the buttons will go. Thread a small needle with about 60 cm of sewing thread, and double it over so you have about 30 cm of doubled thread, then knot the end.
2. Pull the needle through from the back of your paper at the marked spot and up through one hole of the button. Put your needle back in through the other hole of the button and back through your paper at the marked point. Pull the thread firmly. Repeat this three times through each hole of your button.
3. Finish by pushing the thread through to the back of the paper, before pulling the thread tight, thread your needle through the loop of thread then pull tight to form a knot.

BOOK BINDING AND CARD MAKING

Using a craft knife

Before using your craft knife, read the basic safety tips above. When using a craft knife you will also need a cutting mat and a metal ruler. The cutting mat will protect your table surface and stop your project from slipping as you cut. A metal ruler will help prevent your knife from slipping and won't chip when you accidentally cut your ruler instead of your paper.

Before you start you should do a practice run on some scrap paper to let your hand loosen up a bit. Hold the knife in the position that is most comfortable for you: the most common way is as if you were holding a pen. While cutting, hold the paper with your other hand for control and rotate the paper around as you cut. The key is to relax and enjoy the process.

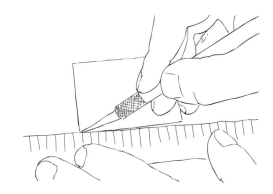

1. Place your card with your drawn or traced design right side up onto your cutting mat. Turn the work so that your metal ruler is covering the drawing and you are cutting on the outside of your design. Place your index finger on the top of the craft knife and hold it as you would a pencil.

2. Begin cutting the paper or card against the ruler with small incremental cuts. If you are cutting freehand and not using a ruler, be sure to keep your hands well away from the knife. You might still like to use the ruler to hold your paper in place and protect your fingers.

3. If you are cutting curves, the trick is to take it slowly. Don't try to cut a long line all at once. If you are cutting out small circles, such as eyes, make short straight cuts around the edge of your circle instead of doing a circular cut.

4. Sometimes you need to go over a line a few times to get a clean cut: don't be tempted to rip away a piece that is not fully cut as you may tear it and ruin all your work.

Scoring paper

Using a bone folder to score lines in heavier papers and card will give your project a clean and professional look. Scoring means making a depression or line into the paper so it can fold more easily. You do this simply by dragging and pressing your bone folder against the ruler line. You can only do this once, so press hard the first time, as it is virtually impossible to score in the same place twice and your paper will show two marks instead of one clean one. If you don't have a bone folder, the dull side of a butter knife will happily do the trick.

SAFETY

Using any kind of tool requires some basic common sense and safe handling; for example, don't leave tools lying around – always put them away after you have finished with them. Here are a few more specific safety tips for your tools:

A craft knife (sometimes called a utility, Stanley or X-ACTO knife) is potentially dangerous to use and requires care and consideration.

- Always remember to retract the blade and replace the safety sleeve after use, and keep the knife in a secure place when not in use.
- Use with a metal ruler and avoid placing your free hand too close to the blade.
- Use slow movements when cutting.
- Point the blade's cutting edge away from your body, and never cut toward the fingers or the hand that is holding the paper.
- It is not necessary to sharpen the blade. Instead, you will need to occasionally replace the old blade with a new one – take care to dispose of the old blade properly.

A sewing machine has a sharp needle going up and down very quickly, so it is important to keep your fingers away from the needle while it is moving.

- Use controlled movements while the machine is running and avoid placing your fingers in front of the needle; instead, guide your object from the side of the needle's path
- Don't look away from the machine while it is running.

An iron can cause burn injuries if you are not careful.

- Iron on a high, stable surface such as an ironing board or table. Don't use the iron on the floor.
- Make sure the electrical cord is out of reach of younger people and is not a tripping hazard.
- Unplug the iron immediately after use. Remember, the iron can take a while to cool down after it is turned off.

Scissors have sharp tips and blades, so you need to be careful to put them away when they are not in use.

- Don't walk around carrying scissors or wave them around while talking.
- Watch where you are cutting, and keep your fingers out of the way.
- Store your scissors in a safe place out of reach.

An awl is a very sharp needle used to poke holes through thick card, leather or layers of paper – always treat it with care.

- Don't leave your awl around for people to play with. Always replace it in its safety sleeve when you are finished with it.
- Always watch where you are poking it. Be careful to protect your table and your hands when you are using it.

Acrylic paints, glitter paints, and glue: there are many types of glues and paints available, so be sure to choose non-toxic and water-based paints and glues for your projects.

- Protect your work surface with newspaper and wear protective clothing such as a plastic apron or old shirt.
- If you do spill paint or glue unexpectedly, clean it up immediately with a warm damp cloth.
- Always clean the nozzle and replace the lid after use so that your paint and glue don't dry out.

play and party

Yay! It's time to have fun, and you can have lots of fun by making things. In this section you will find projects to make and then enjoy playing with for the rest of the day. Using the one-hour paper kite you can find lots of ways to experiment with flight. You can make some paper puppets or a whole bunch of paper animals and then put on a show, or make a super-cute piñata and paper pinwheels for your next party.

Before getting started on these projects, don't forget to first clear your space, gather your materials and read the chapters on safe handling of tools and materials. Ask for help if you need to. Most of the projects in this section need just a few basic items to get started: paper, of course, glue, tape and scissors. There is one project where you will need to use a craft knife and another project requiring a sewing needle and thread. If you don't have these tools or haven't used them before, don't worry: just take a deep breath, relax and give it a go!

aeroplanes

✂

spinning pinwheels

articulated puppets

❀

kites

pet menagerie

monster piñata

🪄

Fly like the wind: Aeroplanes

Explore aerial flight with these two different paper aeroplane designs. Paper aeroplanes are fun to play with: have aeroplane races with your friends, and see whose goes farthest or spins the craziest. They are also a neat way to send messages: write your message on the paper and then fly the plane over to friend on the playground or your mum in the kitchen!

project by: rob shugg
suitable for: beginners
should take: about 1 hour

SHOPPING LIST

- A4 paper in different colours
- Coloured felt-tip markers

CRAFTY NEEDS

- Scissors

NOTES

- Here we have printed designs on the corners of our paper: you can do this or, better yet, draw your own designs with coloured felt-tip markers.
- Flying tips: for your plane to fly smoothly, the wings need to sweep gently upwards.

BASIC START FOR BOTH PLANES

With the design facing down, fold your paper in half lengthways. Then fold the top two corners to the centre fold.

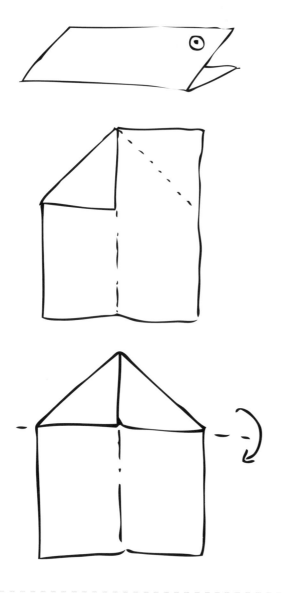

CLASSROOM CLASSIC

1. Begin with the basic start as above, then fold the top point down to the ends of the corners (see diagram 1).

2. Fold the new corners two-thirds of the way down on the centre fold (see diagram 2).

3. Fold the tip up to enclose these flaps (see diagrams 3 and 4).

4. Fold in half again lengthways and make the wings by folding each side down and back up (see diagrams 5 to 7).

5. Cut a notch in the tail with the scissors (see diagram 8).

6. Fold the wings down and push the notched part up (see diagram 9).

7. Optional extras: you could cut small notches in the end of the wings and fold these up or down as you experiment with flying. You could also fold up the wing tips.

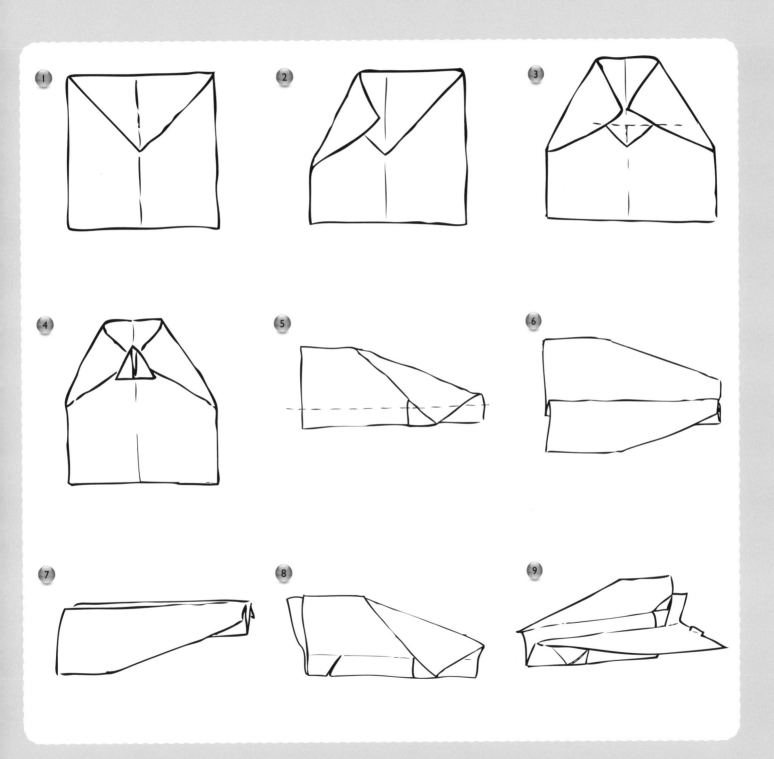

SMOOTH GLIDER

1. Begin with the basic start on page 20, then fold the top point down to just 4 cm from the end of the paper (see diagram 1).

2. Fold the top corners to the centre line (see diagram 2).

3. Then fold the tip up to enclose these flaps (see diagrams 3 and 4).

4. Fold in half lengthways (see diagram 5).

5. Then make the wings by folding each side down to the centre fold (see diagrams 6 to 8).

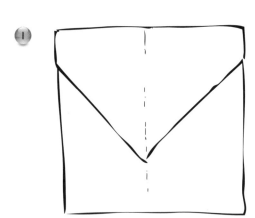

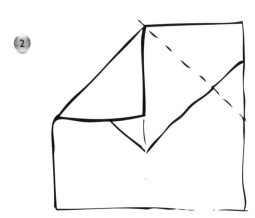

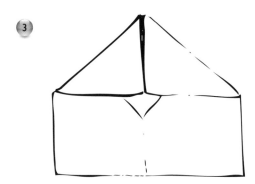

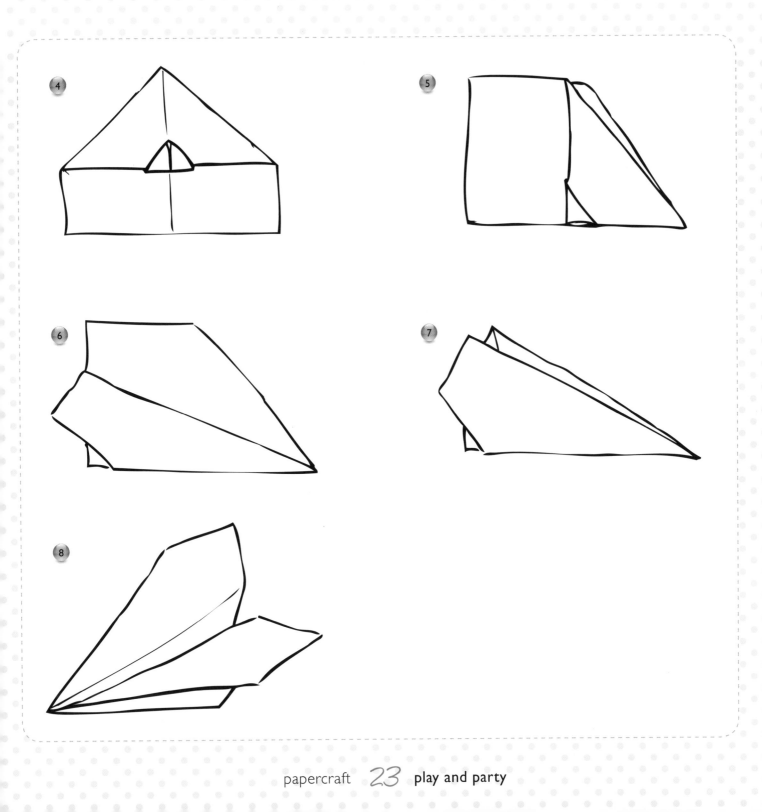

Spinning Pinwheels

On a perfect summer's day spend a bit of the afternoon making a pinwheel from your favourite papers. When you're finished creating, catch a bit of the breeze and watch the vibrant colours whirl about.

project by: olivia kanaley
suitable for: beginners
should take: about 1 hour

SHOPPING LIST

- 7 mm thick wooden dowel, 35 cm long
- Pencil-top eraser (should fit snugly on dowel)
- Paper (double-sided prints look best)
- Sturdy sewing pin, 4 cm long
- Wooden bead

CRAFTY NEEDS

- Scissors
- Pencil
- Glue stick

TEMPLATES

- You will need the Spinning Pinwheels template for this project.

NOTES

- A pencil with an eraser on the end can be used as an alternative to the dowel. Paint your dowels or pencil with acrylic craft paint first if you like.
- Use double-sided scrapbook paper for this project. If you don't have any, you can make double-sided paper by gluing two single-sided printed sheets back to back. This project also works with single-sided paper.
- When poking holes into your paper and eraser, be sure to make the hole large enough for the pinwheel to spin freely. Poke the hole with a sharpened pencil and wiggle it to make the hole bigger.
- There are two variations offered here, the first is simply made from a single piece of paper, cut and folded, while the second requires a template and an extra piece of paper.

FOUR-POINTED PINWHEEL

1. Place the pencil-top eraser on the end of the dowel (see diagram 1). Set aside.

2. Cut out a small star from paper using the template provided, poke the pin through it and set it aside (see diagram 2).

3. Cut a square of paper 15 x 15 cm. Fold it in half diagonally, unfold and then repeat on the other side so your square has an 'X' across it (see diagram 3). Poke a hole in the centre of the 'X' with a sharpened pencil.

4. Use a ruler to mark 3 cm from the centre point along the folded lines towards each corner, then take your scissors and cut inward from each corner along the fold, stopping at the 3 cm mark. Poke holes in every second triangular point (see diagram 4).

5. Bring each point with a hole in it to the centre of the pinwheel and thread them onto the pin one by one. Then poke the pin through the hole you made earlier at the back of the pinwheel (in the centre of the 'X').

6. Thread a bead onto the pin before poking it into the eraser on top of the dowel (see diagram 5).

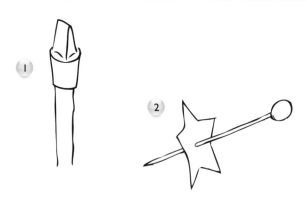

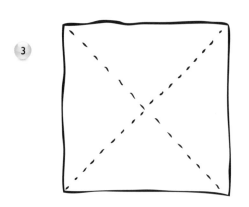

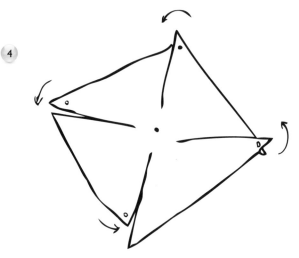

EIGHT-POINTED PINWHEEL

1. Place the pencil-top eraser on the end of the dowel (see diagram 1). Set aside.

2. Cut out a small paper star from paper using the template provided, poke the pin through it and set it aside (see diagram 2).

3. Trace the template provided onto two different 20 cm-square pieces of patterned paper and cut both of them out using scissors. Poke holes where the template shows.

4. Place the cut-outs on top of each other and stagger them so you can see all eight points (see diagram 6). Glue them together at the centre.

5. Thread a pin through each of the eight holes in the 'spokes', working your way around the circle one by one. Then poke the pin through to the back of the pinwheel. Thread a bead onto the pin before poking it into the eraser on top of the dowel (see diagram 5).

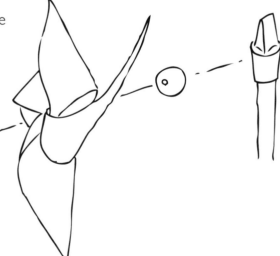

Articulated Puppets

These two paper puppets are simple to make, yet fun and satisfying. Once you get the hang of the general principle, you can experiment and adapt these ideas to all sorts of different designs. You could make them all afternoon!

project by: rob shugg
suitable for: beginners
should take: 1–2 hours

SHOPPING LIST

- Paint colour sample cards
- Small brads

CRAFTY NEEDS

- Small hole puncher
- Scissors

TEMPLATES

- You will need the Articulated Puppet template for this project.

NOTES

- **'Wobbles':** the wobbly headed robot has parallelogram legs and a neck shaped like a cross. This means that Wobbles can shuffle along by moving the legs up and down and his head will move about randomly – it can even do a complete 360-degree turn.
- **'Extendo':** the extendable jaws are based on a scissor lift, where linked, folding supports are structured in an 'X' pattern. Push from the lower supports to push Extendo up to his full height.
- **Paint colour sample cards:** the big ones are used here. You can get them for free from the paint section of a hardware store. We love using paint colour sample cards because they come in so many wonderful bright colours and are just the right weight for many projects. You can also use card stock or any medium-weight card.

1. Trace and cut out templates

Choose which puppet you would like to make, and trace the template onto the paint sample cards. Cut out the paint sample cards using the templates provided (see diagram 1).

2. Punch holes

Punch holes where marked on the templates (see diagram 2).

3. Join pieces together

Join the pieces together using the brads (see diagrams 3 and 4). Don't make the brads too tight as the joints need to be able to move freely.

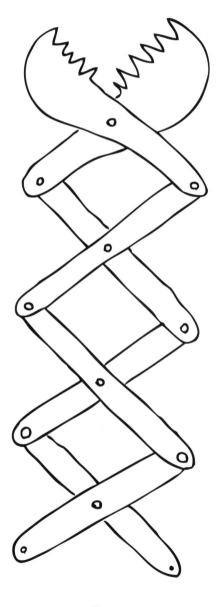

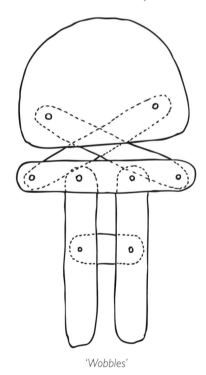

'Wobbles'

'Extendo'

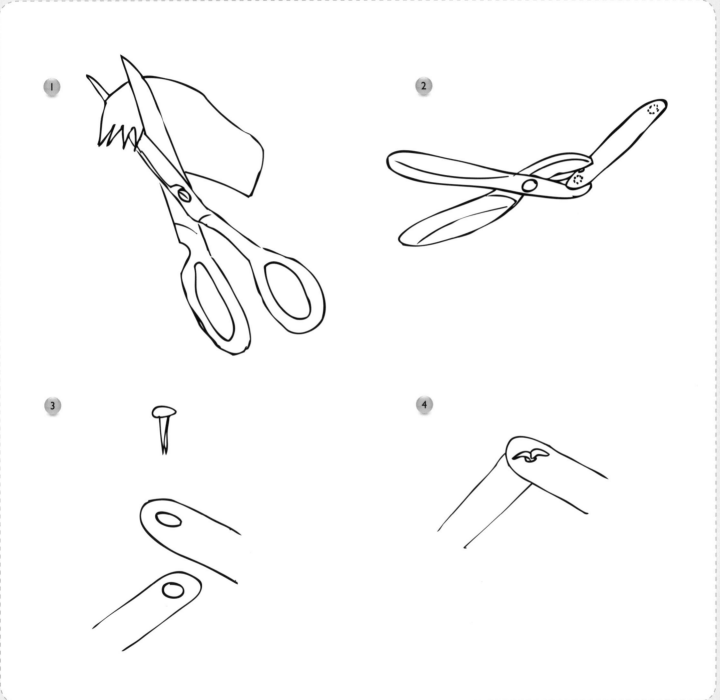

Up, up and away: Kites

This little paper kite is surprisingly effective at flying. Make it in an hour or two and then spend the afternoon at the park, flying it with your parents or your friends.

project by: rob shugg
suitable for: confident beginners
should take: 2–3 hours

SHOPPING LIST

- Gift-wrapping paper or brown craft paper
- Long bamboo barbecue skewers
- Cotton twine
- Small wooden bead
- Ribbon

CRAFTY NEEDS

- Scissors
- Ruler
- Pencil
- Butter knife or bone folder
- Glue

NOTES

- You can make this kite twice as big by joining two barbecue skewers together. To do this, overlap the skewers in the centre and wrap twine around them.

1. Make the cross frame

Take your two long barbecue skewers and remove the pointy ends with the scissors. Measure and mark the halfway point on one, and the two-thirds point on the other. Lash them together at these points with cotton string and a drop of glue (see diagram 1).

2. Form the frame

Cut a very small notch in the end of each skewer. Tie twine around the end of one skewer and secure with glue (see diagram 2), then thread it through each skewer end notch until it forms a diamond shape around the skewer cross. Pull the twine taut enough so it holds its shape, but not so tight that it warps the skewers. Tie it off at the end and secure with another drop of glue. This forms your kite frame.

3. Cut out the paper

Lay your paper down so the good side is facing downwards – it should be about 2 cm bigger on all sides than your kite frame. Lay your kite frame on top of the paper and, with your pencil, mark a dot at each point of the frame. Remove the frame and draw a line between the dots with your ruler and pencil. Then draw a parallel line 1 cm bigger on all sides. Cut out the kite shape on the outer line with scissors.

4. Fold the paper

Cut out notches from the corners of the paper (see diagram 3). Score the inner line with your ruler and a butter knife and then fold this inwards.

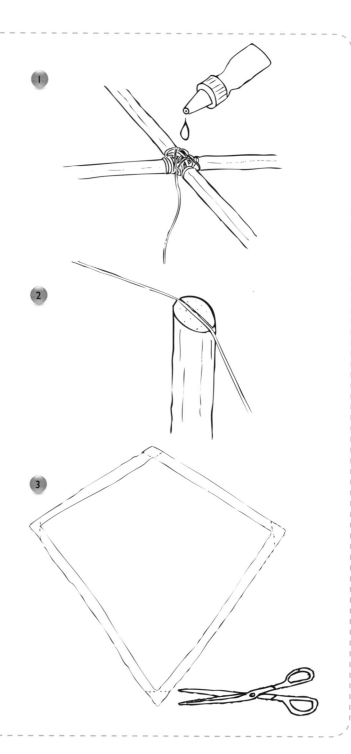

5. Glue the paper over the frame

Place the kite frame onto the back of the paper in position and, using only a small amount of glue, fold each edge of paper over the twine and stick down, holding each one for a minute or until the glue sets (see diagram 4). Add an extra dab of glue on the corners of the paper to stick them down over the skewers.

6. Attach the string

Measure the long skewer and add an extra 15 cm, then cut a piece of cotton twine to this length. Tie one end to the top of the long skewer then, about a third of the way down the string, loop it through the bead (see diagram 5). Tie the other end of the string to the bottom end of the long skewer. Add a drop of glue to each of the knots to secure them into position.

7. Decorate the kite tail

Cut about 10 small paper bows or cloud shapes from matching paper. Take a length of thin ribbon (about 2 m) and tape your bows or cloud-shaped decorations onto the ribbon at 30 cm intervals. Tape, tie or glue the end of the ribbon onto the bottom end of the long skewer (see diagram 6).

8. Get ready to fly

Measure about 10 metres of cotton twine and wrap it around a piece of cardboard or three ice-block sticks glued together. Tie the end of the cotton twine onto the bead. Now go and fly your kite!

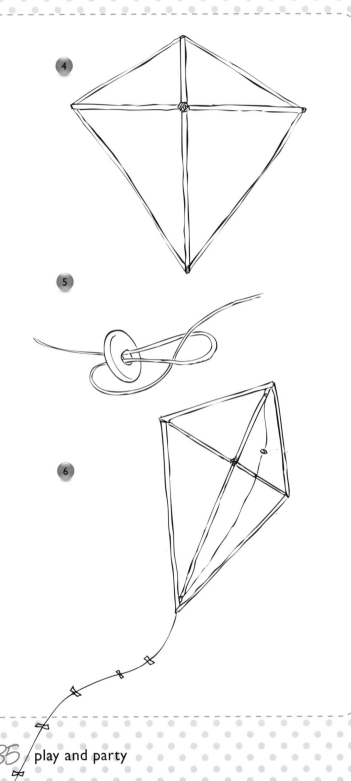

Pet Menagerie

Have you always wanted a kitten or your very own puppy dog? Here's a pet that won't bark at the neighbours or chase mice while you're trying to sleep. This paper pet will sit on your desk or nightstand and keep you company, and it never needs to be fed or taken to the vet. Make a whole litter!

project by: nancy w. hall
suitable for: confident beginners
should take: an afternoon

SHOPPING LIST

- Decorative paper, such as road maps, comic-book pages, wrapping paper, brown paper bags
- 1 m medium-weight fusible white interfacing (available at fabric stores)
- Pillow stuffing
- 2 to 4 colourful buttons
- Embroidery thread that matches or contrasts with your paper
- Snack-sized zip-lock plastic bag containing a handful of clean sand, bird-seed, or uncooked rice for weight
- 2 coins and some clear sticky tape
- Large envelope

CRAFTY NEEDS

- Scissors
- Embroidery needle
- Thimble
- Ironing board
- Iron
- 5 small binder clips
- Chopstick

TECHNIQUES

- Using fusible interfacing, page 12
- Hand sewing, page 12
- Sewing a button, page 13

TEMPLATES

- You will need the Pet Menagerie template for this project.

NOTES

- Trace or photocopy the templates onto paper and cut them out. For a cat, you will need the pieces for the cat body, cat tail, cat ears and cat base. For a dog, you will need the pieces for the dog body, dog tail, dog ears and dog base. After you cut out the pattern pieces, slip them into an envelope to keep them safe so that you can use them another time.
- When a note on a pattern piece tells you to cut 2 (such as on the tails), cut one with the pattern piece facing up and the other with the piece facing down, so you end up with pieces that are mirror images of each other. When a pattern piece tells you to cut out four pieces (two for each ear), cut two with the pattern face up and two with the pattern face down.
- The stitching on this project can be done by hand or with a sewing machine.
- If you want your dog's ears to flop down, use a little tape to attach a small coin to the underside of each one.

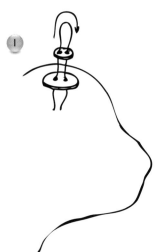

1. Prepare the paper

For each animal cut out three pieces of interfacing and three pieces of your decorative paper so that they're all the same size as a piece of regular copy paper (A4). Set your iron at a medium setting (no steam) and iron your paper flat. Place a piece of fusible interfacing, rough (sticky) side down, onto the back of each piece of paper and use your iron to adhere the interfacing to the back of each piece of paper.

2. Cut out the pattern pieces

Arrange your pattern pieces onto the three pieces of interfacing-backed paper so that they all fit, and cut out each piece following the instructions on the templates.

3. Sew on the eyes

Using a needle and thread, sew a button for an eye onto each of the animal body pieces (see diagram 1).

4. Make the tail and ears

Place the two tail pieces together, with right sides facing out. Place the four ear pieces together in the same way, so you have two ears. Hold each pair together with small binder clips. Use your needle and embroidery thread to stitch all the way around the sides of the tail and each ear. For the puppy ears: at the straight edge of each ear, fold down 2 cm and place the ears in matching positions on each side of the head. Stitch the turned-down part of the ear to the body (see diagram 2). For the cat ears: fold the ears in half and tuck them into the seam at the top of the head (see diagram 3).

5. Sew it all together

Place the two body pieces together, with right sides facing outwards and hold them together with the binder clips. Insert the straight-edged end of the tail between the body front and body back pieces, positioning it at a pleasing angle, and hold with another binder clip. Stitch around the outside of your animal, leaving the base open. When you come to the tail, continue sewing through all four layers. If you are having trouble, use a thimble to help you to push the needle through.

6. Stuff the animal

Take a small handful of stuffing and stuff it into the head first, using a chopstick to poke more stuffing in a little at a time until there is only about 4 cm of space left at the open end. Lay the zip-lock bag with its contents in the open end, on top of the stuffing: this will help your pet to stand up nicely. Place the base piece, with right side facing outwards, over the base opening and use binder clips to hold it in place while you stitch around the base (see diagram 4).

Monster Piñata

Make a monster from cereal boxes for your next party! But beware – these piñatas may be too cute for whacking with a stick.

project by: teri dimalanta
suitable for: beginners
should take: 1–2 hours

SHOPPING LIST

• Cereal or cracker boxes
• Coloured tissue paper
• Craft paper and other decorations
• Fine wire (optional)

CRAFTY NEEDS

• Glue
• Masking tape
• Scissors

NOTES

• Collect cereal or biscuit boxes to make your monster piñata – the size of the box determines the size of your monster.

1. Prepare your boxes

Look for boxes that are undamaged, then undo the top opening and cut rounded corners on the front and back of the cereal box, but leave the side flaps uncut (see diagram 1). Tape these side flaps over onto your curved shape to create a closed curved top to your box.

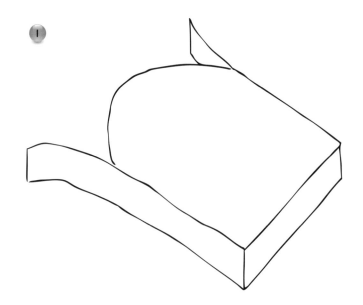

2. Prepare your strips of tissue paper fringing

Cut your coloured tissue paper into 10 cm-wide strips. Stack them on top of each other and make vertical cuts 1 cm apart, and about half way through the fringing (see diagram 2).

3. Glue on strips of fringing

Use your glue to attach the fringing onto your box. Start at the bottom and work your way up to the top, overlapping your strips slightly so that the fringing will layer (see diagram 3). You might like to alternate your colours or use the same colour on the bottom half and switch colours for the top half.

4. Decorate your monster

Once the fringes have been glued down, you can decorate your monster with coloured craft paper to make its eyes, mouth, ears, bowtie, belt – whatever you can come up with. Use the photos and diagrams 4 and 5 as a guide to inspire you!

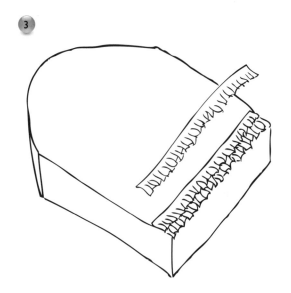

3

5. Add a hanging loop
If you want to hang your guy somewhere, attach a little fine wire to the top of his head with tape, then cover this with more fringing to hide the tape.

4

5

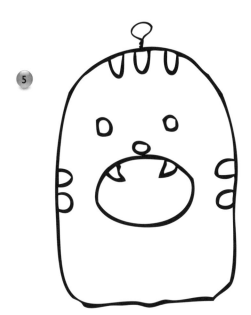

be an individual

Are you a collector? A bookworm? A budding writer? Do you like to be an individual, and surround yourself with your stuff? This chapter has projects such as making your own book to keep your secret thoughts or share them with friends, as well as a cool bookmark to use with your special book. You can also make use of some of your collected treasures with some collage projects like the Collage Letters and the Shadow Box. If you want to personalise your room or your outfit, try making some stencil art or paper beads.

Before getting started on these projects, get organised! Gather your materials. Read the sections on safe handling of tools and equipment, and ask for help if you need it. Most of the projects in this section need just a few basic items to get started: paper, of course, glue, tape and scissors. There is one project that will require the use of a craft knife and another project for which a needle and thread will come in handy, but if you don't have these tools or haven't used them before, don't worry. Read the instructions and check with your parents first: you might need a little help to get started, but after that you should be fine on your own.

stitch-bound book

confidential pocket book

book invaders

a string of beads

under-the-sea stencils

collage letters

papier-mâché owls

shadow box

Stitch-bound Book

A blank book is a handy thing when inspiration strikes. There is no better place to record your ideas, dreams, secrets, stories and adventures. Learn this basic bookbinding technique, and you will be able to publish as many books as you can imagine, using almost any materials you have on hand. As a book-maker and as an author, the possibilities are endless!

project by: jennifer hallissy
suitable for: beginners
should take: about 1 hour

SHOPPING LIST

- Light-weight cardboard for book cover (cereal boxes work well)
- String, twine or embroidery thread
- Paper for book pages
- Decorative paper, photo, or image for book cover
- Blank labels

CRAFTY NEEDS

- Straight-edge ruler
- Pencil
- Scissors
- 2 binder clips
- Small hole puncher
- Awl
- Blunt-tipped embroidery needle

TEMPLATES

- You can use the Stitch-bound Book template for this project if you need to.

NOTES

- The pages of this book can be made with many different types of paper, including blank paper, lined paper, graph paper, recycled printer paper, brown paper bags … see what you have around and be resourceful!
- Be particularly careful when using an awl – it can be quite sharp. If you find it tricky to poke through all the pages with this tool, you might want to tap the end of your awl gently with a hammer to help you along.
- If you don't have an awl you could use a nail and hammer. Hammer the nail through, where indicated, onto a block of wood outside, not onto your dining room table!

1. Make the book cover

Use a ruler and pencil to draw a 12 x 25 cm rectangle onto your card, then use scissors to cut it out. Firmly crease it down the middle to make the front and back cover.

2. Prepare the pages

Use a ruler and pencil to draw 10 x 23 cm rectangles onto your paper, then use scissors to cut it out. About six to ten pages is a good number to begin with. Firmly crease the pages down the middle. Centre your pages inside your cover, lining them all up at the creases. Close your book and clamp the cover and pages together securely with binder clips.

3. Pierce the stitching holes

To make four evenly spaced holes down the spine of your book, first use your ruler and pencil to draw a vertical line 1.5 cm to the right of the spine. Then, make marks down your vertical line every 2.5 cm. These marks indicate where the holes will be punched. You can also use the hole template: copy it onto paper and use a hole puncher to punch out the holes where indicated. Place this template on top of your book and make a mark with your pencil where each hole is. Using the awl (or hammer and nail), carefully poke through your cover and pages where you made your marks in order to create four holes.

4. Sew the book together

Cut a piece of string or thread about 120 cm long. Thread this through the needle, leaving about 20 cm of string hanging on one side of the needle. Tie a knot on the end of the long side of the string. Pierce your needle through the middle crease of your pages, about 5 cm from the bottom and pull your string all the way through (this secures the knot of the thread in the middle of the book). Push your needle through hole #3 from the inside of the cover. Refer to binding diagrams 1 to 8 to continue sewing up your book binding. Remember to pull the string snug as you sew.

5. Decorate the book

Cut out some decorative paper, a picture or an image to embellish your book cover. Add a label, and you're ready to write!

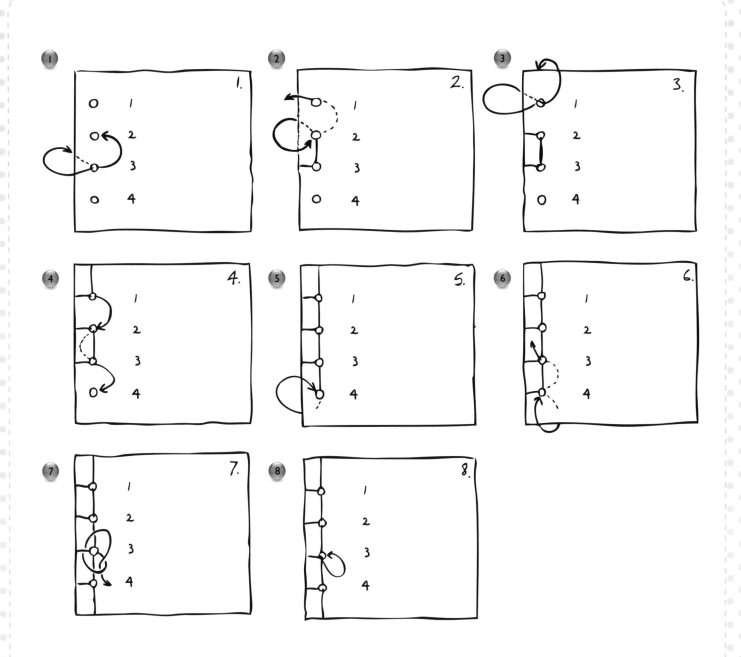

Confidential Pocket Book

Is it a journal ... or is it a place to stash collectables and notes? This easy version of the classic accordion book stretches out to reveal hidden treasures and a place to write. Take it with you wherever you go.

project by: nancy w. hall
suitable for: confident beginners
should take: about 1 hour

SHOPPING LIST

- 2 letter-sized file folders, plain, coloured, or patterned; select one with its labelling tab at either end of the folder instead of in the centre
- 45 cm of string, waxed linen thread, narrow ribbon or cord
- Slightly stiff paper or card stock for the covers and optional decoration
- A button to match or contrast with your cover paper
- Embellishments of your choice, such as rubber stamps, paper scraps, beads, embroidery thread, stickers, exotic postage stamps
- 4 or 5 sheets of white copy paper

CRAFTY NEEDS

- Scissors
- Ruler
- Glue stick
- Pencil
- Hole puncher
- Spoon, butter knife or bone folder
- Stapler
- Large needle

TECHNIQUES

- Adding buttons, page 13

NOTES

- This book is like a blank canvas for you to experiment with. It could be a nature or dream journal, or a place to keep your collectible cards. Your paper – take-away menus, plain paper to draw or stamp on, or postcards from a friend – will guide you as you design a book that's all about you.

1. Cut and score the folder

Lay the folder closed on the table with its folded edge to your left. Lightly draw a line one-third of the way up and cut along this line, discard the bottom one-third piece. Now open this book shape and use a bone folder or butter knife to score a line 7 cm up from the bottom edge that you cut. Then fold along your scored line up toward the top of the folder (see diagram 1). Use the back of a spoon or bone folder to press and smooth the fold. The book should look as if there is a wide pocket along the bottom. Now open the pocket back out again.

2. Make the accordion shape

Fold the left and right edges of the book to the centre fold. Crease these folded edges neatly with your spoon or bone folder, then open the book again. One more time, open up the book and again fold the bottom part back up along the fold line you made before (see diagram 2). Holding that fold in place, fold along all the vertical lines so that the book makes a sort of zigzag shape – just like an accordion – with pockets along the inside (see diagram 3).

3. Create covers

Lay the folded book on top of your decorative paper and trace around it to make two rectangles the same size as the book. Cut these out and glue these covers to the front and back of the book, to make it stronger and neater. Set this aside to dry while you make a little journal.

4. Make a journal

Take the discarded piece from your file folder and cut a book shape out of it as you did before, only smaller – closed, it should measure about 10.5 cm tall and 8.5 cm wide. Open the book up and glue a piece of decorative paper to the outside, smoothing out any wrinkles in the paper. Carefully fold the book shape again (with the decorated side on the outside) while the glue is still damp – it will fit the book better. Lay your stack of copy paper on the table and fold lengthwise, then cut out pages for the book, making sure the folded edge will act like the spine of the book. At the other edge of the copy paper, cut another set of pages. Nest the pages inside the little book's cover, trimming them with scissors just a little to make them fit inside the cover. Now, hold the book open, with its pages in place, and staple right into the spine twice, near the top and bottom (see diagram 4).

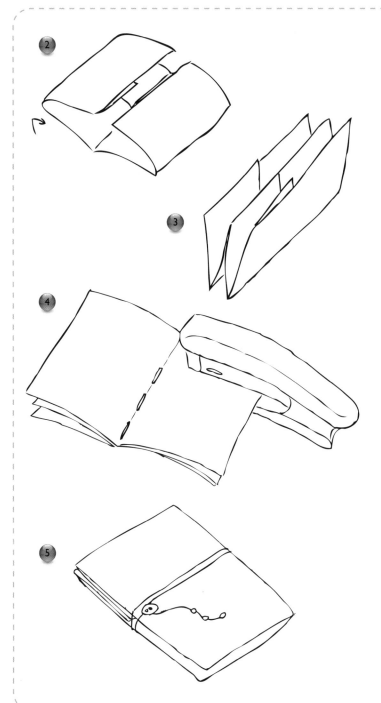

5. Finishing

With the closed accordion on the table in front of you, find a spot near the right edge of the cover where a doorknob would be if the book were a door. On the inside of the cover (you might have to open the pocket edge a little), use a heavy needle to make two holes close together at this spot. Thread a button onto the string and hold it in place on the outside of the book cover while you pull the ends of the string through the two holes and back inside the book. One end will be long, the other only about 8 cm. Tie the ends of the string together using a reef knot (loop the left end of the string over the right end and then loop the right end over the left to make a non-slip knot) and thread the long end of the string (carefully) back into one hole so it comes out on the outside (don't trim it). Trim the short inside thread.

6. Decorate your book

Now it's time to decorate your mini book and the cover of your secret pocket book. Place the little book in one of the pockets, and wrap the cord twice around the closed book and then twice around the button to keep it closed (see diagram 5). Be prepared to help your friends make journals for themselves – everyone will want one when they see yours!

Book Invaders

These cut-and-fold book invader bookmarks are based on a combination of Japanese kirigami and origami techniques, resulting in a cool 3D bookmark. It's a relatively simple project that only requires patience and careful work. Once you have this down, you won't stop at making just one.

project by: elod beregszaszi
suitable for: confident beginners
should take: less than 1 hour

SHOPPING LIST

- Heavy-weight card stock in various colours
- 1 sheet dressmaker's carbon paper

CRAFTY NEEDS

- Cutting mat
- Craft knife
- Ruler

TEMPLATES

- You will need the Book Invaders template for this project.

NOTES

- This project requires good, precise cutting skills with a craft knife, so be sure to read the safety instructions on page 14 before you start.

1. Trace the template onto your card stock

Trace with carbon paper or photocopy your template directly onto your card stock, being sure to note which lines you need to cut and where you need to fold. Fold the card stock in half lengthways down the dotted line on the template (see diagram 1).

2. Cut the shapes

Using a craft knife, ruler and cutting mat, cut carefully along the cutting lines, making sure you do not cut where there are spaces marked between the cutting lines (see diagram 2). This is a tricky process, so take your time.

3. Pop up the shape

Take the cut-out and, while pushing out the space invader character at the top from behind, push down on the centre fold with your other hand to pop out your shape (see diagrams 3 and 4).

4. Finishing

Finally, flatten the bookmark again. Press down on your collapsed bookmark and lightly go over the crease lines with your fingers.

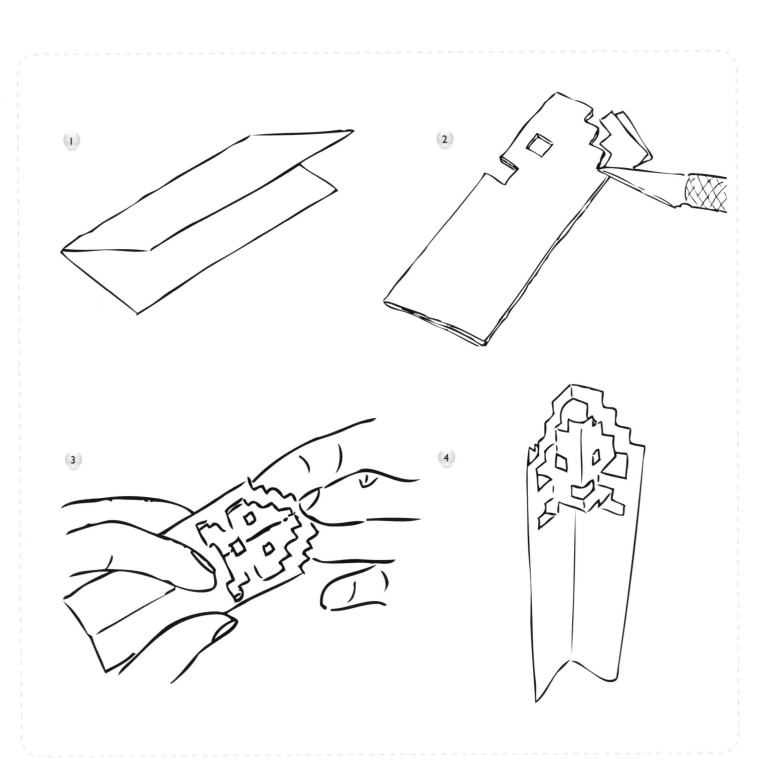

A String of Beads

Paper beads are addictive to make and allow you to add a personal touch to your jewellery and accessories. Making beads is fun, and you can recycle papers to make gorgeous gifts for friends and family.

project by: kathreen ricketson
suitable for: beginners
should take: 1–2 hours, depending on how many you are making

SHOPPING LIST

- Colourful paper, copy paper, magazine pages or scrapbooking paper
- PVA craft glue
- Sheets of newspaper to protect your table

CRAFTY NEEDS

- Ruler
- Pencil
- Scissors
- Paintbrush
- Barbecue skewers

TEMPLATES

- Make a template by using a ruler and pencil – draw a long thin triangle on card and cut it out. The triangle can be any length, up to the length of your paper or magazine pages, and should be about 2–4 cm wide at the blunt end, tapering to a point at the other end.
- Make different-shaped beads by varying the shape of your triangle. Try a shorter, fatter triangle or a long, thin rectangle that tapers to a point in the last 5 cm.

NOTES

- You can thread these beads onto elastic, wire, string or leather and tie the ends to make necklaces, bracelets, or even a door curtain. Alternate them with glass or plastic beads for a different look.
- Add glitter to your final glue coating for a shimmery bead, or make the beads from plain paper and draw a design on!

1. Cut the paper shapes

Trace your template onto paper and cut out. Draw around this template on the wrong side of your colourful paper using your ruler and pencil. Cut out along the marked lines of your paper with scissors (see diagram 1). You will need one long, pointed triangle (or other shape) for every bead you wish to make.

2. Apply glue

Lay out your newspaper to protect your table, then apply glue (using a paintbrush if you wish) onto the pointed end of the wrong side of your cut-out paper pieces (see diagram 2). Apply the glue about three quarters of the way along the triangle, leaving about 10 cm at the wide end unglued.

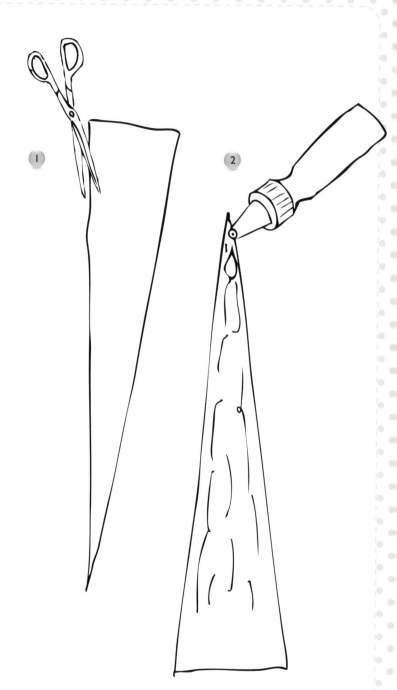

3. Roll the beads

Take your barbecue skewer and begin to roll the wide end of the paper onto the skewer, holding the paper so that the glued side faces you (see diagram 3). Ensure you keep the paper symmetrical as you are rolling – this can take a bit of practice at first. Finish rolling the paper all the way up, keeping the pointy end centred.

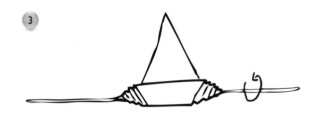

4. Finishing

Finish your bead with a final coating of glue all over, to strengthen the bead and give it a bit of a shine. You could add some glitter into your glue for this final coating if you like. Thread your beads onto skewers and leave them to dry standing upright in a ball of Blu-Tack (see diagram 4). They will need to dry overnight to completely harden before you can use them.

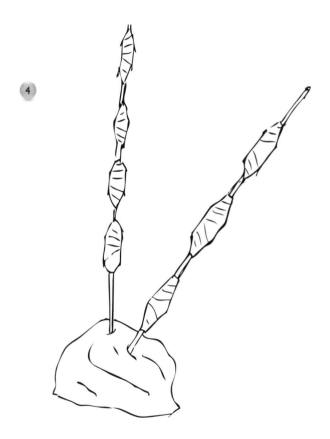

Under-the-Sea Stencils

These stencils can be placed anywhere you like. Here they are painted onto canvas frames, but you could stencil T-shirts or plain cotton bags with fabric paints or – with your parents' permission – you could even stencil your bedroom walls.

project by: kathreen ricketson
suitable for: confident beginners
should take: 2–3 hours or the whole afternoon

SHOPPING LIST

- Canvas, paper or fabric to place your design (canvas frames are available at craft and art supply stores)
- Freezer paper
- Acrylic paints (if putting your design on a T-shirt or bag, you will need fabric paints)

CRAFTY NEEDS

- Craft knife
- Cutting mat
- Foam paint roller and plastic tray
- Iron
- Pencil

TEMPLATES

- You will need the Under-the-Sea Stencils template for this project.

NOTES

- Before starting, prepare your paper or canvas by painting your background colours, if you like, and let them dry completely.
- If you have never used a craft knife or done any intricate paper cutting before, begin with the simpler design of the whale first.
- If you are careful you can use your stencil a couple of times before it becomes too clogged with paint to be usable.
- If you are creating a complex design with several layers of stencil, wait until each layer of paint is dry before applying the next stencil.

1. Trace the templates

Cut a piece of freezer paper big enough for your design, being sure to leave at least a 20 cm perimeter around your design. Trace the templates onto the rough side of your freezer paper (see diagram 1).

2. Cut out shapes

With your cutting mat on the table, use your craft knife to carefully cut out your stencil design on the marked lines (see diagram 2). Do this slowly and carefully without rushing. Take lots of breaks and deep breaths.

3. Apply the stencil

Once you have cut out your design completely, place your freezer-paper stencil smooth (waxy) side down onto your paper, canvas or T-shirt, take a hot iron and carefully iron the freezer paper in place (see diagram 3). The smooth side of the paper contains a wax that will adhere to fabric with heat but will peel off very easily. Make sure all the bits are pressed in place and there are no edges curling up.

4. Paint

Roll a little paint onto your foam roller – not too much – and take it slowly as you build up the thickness of paint, rather than painting it thickly in one go. Gently roll the paint over the design, a little at a time, being careful not to lift up the edges of your stencil (see diagram 4). If you want your paint to be thicker, wait for a few minutes for the first coat of paint to dry before applying a new coat. Once you are satisfied, let your design dry for a few minutes, but not completely, before carefully peeling away the stencil.

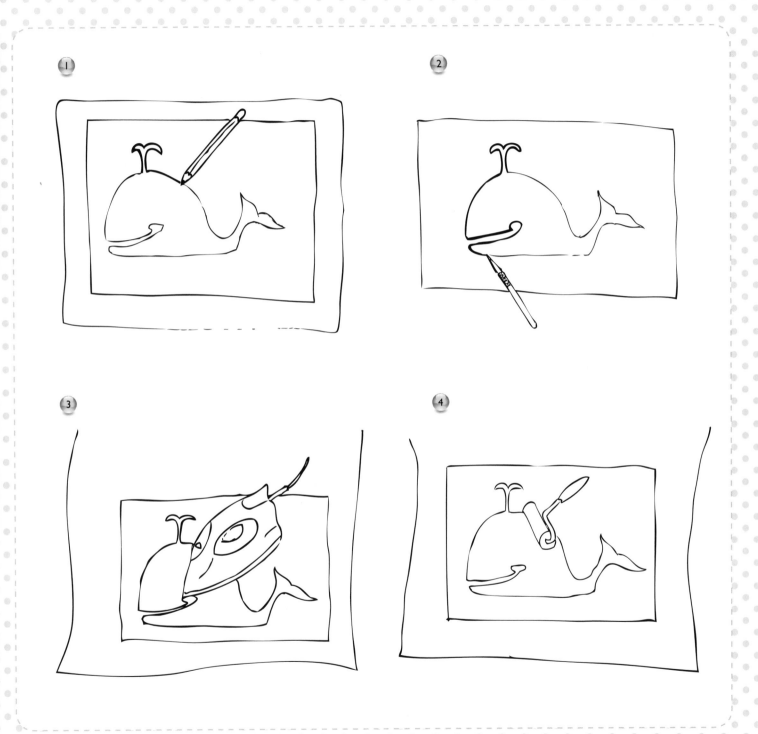

Collage Letters

When you've got something to say, why not say it in a BIG way? In this project, mixed-media collage and oversized alphabet letters combine to create the ultimate personal statement. Self-expression never looked so good!

project by: jennifer hallissy
suitable for: beginners
should take: 2–3 hours

SHOPPING LIST

- Papier-mâché, wood, or MDF pre-cut letters from craft store
- Assorted paper, such as original drawings, old homework, photos, comic book or catalogue pages, magazine pictures, scrapbooking paper, gift wrap, sheet music, ticket stubs, postcards, stamps and stickers, letters from your pen pal – you name it!
- PVA or decoupage glue

CRAFTY NEEDS

- Scissors
- Paintbrush

NOTES

- Instead of purchasing pre-cut letters from the craft store, you can cut large letters from thick cardboard for this project. You might like to print out large letters in your favourite font and use these as a template to cut your own letters from cardboard boxes.
- This project is a great way to showcase your collection of keepsakes and souvenirs, so, before starting, go on a hunt and gather up all of those special little somethings that you just can't bear to part with (fortunes from fortune cookies, ticket stubs, a favourite comic strip).

1. Gather the materials

Assemble all the interesting bits and pieces of paper that you can find. If you need to add to your collection, flip through old magazines and catalogues, cutting out cool pictures and words as they catch your eye. You could also print or photocopy favourite photos.

2. Decide on your design

Decide where on your letter shape you want to place each piece of paper, and trim it with the scissors until it fits (see diagram 1).

3. Stick it all down

Attach one image at a time by applying a thin layer of glue to the back of your paper with a paintbrush and stick it on to your letter (see diagram 2). Glue down any large or background pieces first. Keep gluing paper, pictures, words and other items to the front of your letter shape until the entire surface is covered. It is okay to overlap and layer papers on top of each other.

4. Finishing

Once you have finished your collage, let the glue dry for 20–30 minutes. Brush a final thin layer of glue over the entire surface. Let it dry overnight. You can make just one letter, your whole name, or an entire sentence, then hang the letters on your wall or stand them on your windowsill or bookcase.

Papier-mâché Owls

These cute owl ornaments are made using a simple cheat's papier-mâché method where the boring part of building the layers and shape is easy and quick, leaving more time for the fun part: decorating!

project by: lisa tilse
suitable for: beginners
should take: about 2 hours

SHOPPING LIST

- Broadsheet newspaper (this is a large newspaper, at least 60 cm tall)
- Coloured and patterned light- to medium-weight papers, such as origami paper, magazine pages, wrapping paper
- Sticky tape
- PVA glue

CRAFTY NEEDS

- Scissors
- Paintbrush
- Pen or pencil
- Plastic lid

TEMPLATES

- You will need the Papier-mâché Owls template for this project.

NOTES

- Use both patterned and plain papers, and choose papers that have some colours in common for each owl.
- The size of your owls will vary depending on your newspaper size and how tightly you wrap your owl's body. You may need to adjust the size of the template pieces for the wings and eyes so they look in proportion on your owl. The instructions given here fit an owl about 7.5 cm high. To make a baby owl (5 cm high) use newspaper half the size.
- You can use the same oval shape as the owl's body to create lots of different creatures: rabbits, cats, dogs, even robots or people. Simply adjust the ear shape and placement and draw on a different face!

1. Make the body

Take one page of newspaper and scrunch it up into a tight ball. Flatten it out, then scrunch it up again (see diagram 1). The paper will become very soft. Scrunch and flatten about six times, and finish with it scrunched up in a tight ball. Use sticky tape to secure the newspaper into the oval shape of your owl.

2. Wrap the body

Take a quarter of a newspaper page and scrunch and flatten until the paper is soft. Flatten it out and wrap this flattened piece tightly around your scrunched up ball to make a hard solid shape with a smooth surface. Use tape to secure it and refine the shape. Your owl should be an oval with a flattened base so it can stand on its own.

3. Papier-mâché

Cut the coloured paper into 1 x 1.5 cm pieces. You will also need some smaller pieces and some strips about 0.5 x 2 cm. Paint PVA glue on a quarter of your owl and place the pretty paper pieces on so that they overlap (see diagram 2). Each time you add a piece of paper, paint glue over it, so the next piece will stick when it overlaps. The PVA will dry clear, so it's better to use too much than not enough. The smaller pieces will cover any little gaps and the longer strips are good for wrapping around the bottom and top edges. Continue until you've covered the sides and the bottom (see diagram 3).

Put the owl on its head to dry a little, then cover the top and allow to dry in the sun. It doesn't need to be completely dry, but it will be easier to handle.

4. Add wings and features

Trace or copy the template pieces onto plain paper and cut them out. Place your templates on some good paper and trace around them. Cut out each piece. You should have one beak, four wings, six eyes, one face, one chest and two feet. Glue the beak onto the face triangle, then glue it onto your owl so the outer points of the triangle stick out (see diagram 4). Glue the parts of the eyes together and paint PVA on one half of the backs of the eyes. Stick them onto the owl so the outer sides stick out.

5. Assemble the owl

Cut the chest piece where the dotted lines are, and glue each piece in place onto the owl, overlapping them slightly so they fit around the curve of the owl's body. The outer shape of the chest piece should form an oval. Paint PVA on the top wing points and glue them onto the owl so that the rest of the wings are not touching the body.

6. Finishing

Glue the feet under the owl. Attach a small rectangle of the paper you used for the body over the join to reinforce it. Add embellishments like paper flowers or leaves (see diagram 5), then allow to dry overnight.

Shadow Box

Shadow boxes are a great way to get special things out of the drawer and on display. They would also make a great gift for your best friend with photos of the two of you and reminders of special things you've done together.

project by: lisa tilse
suitable for: beginners
should take: 1–2 hours

SHOPPING LIST

- Boxes of various sizes: cereal boxes, shoe boxes, gift boxes
- Coloured and patterned papers: origami paper, magazine pages, gift wrap
- Double-sided tape
- Velcro dots with sticky backs
- Small cardboard pieces
- Things you want to display: photos, cards, tickets, small toys, ornaments

CRAFTY NEEDS

- Scissors
- Craft knife
- Cutting mat
- Ruler
- Pencil

NOTES

- Use PVA craft glue to collage smaller pieces of paper onto the inside and outsides of your box for a different look.
- Vary the size of the objects you are displaying. Use the whole depth of the box – put objects in the background and foreground. Rather than sticking something to the back wall of the box, give the illusion that it's floating by bringing it forward.
- Don't try to fit too many things in one shadow box. Simpler is usually better. If you want to display a small collection you could work out a grid and lay them out in rows.
- A group of shadow boxes will work better if they have some elements in common. Repeat a colour, paper or shape (for example, circular objects) in two or more boxes. Start with three or five boxes.
- Paint a craftwood alphabet letter for your assemblage and make mini bunting from string and triangles of coloured paper.

1. Cover the box

Place your coloured or patterned paper right side down onto your cutting mat and position your box on top. Trace around the base of the box (see diagram 1). Roll it over onto one side and trace around the side (see diagram 2). Repeat for all sides (see diagram 3). Your traced areas should form a cross shape. Then add tabs, 1 cm wide, and an additional 1.5 cm around the top edges (see diagram 4). Cut the shape out with a craft knife and a ruler (or scissors). Stick double-sided tape on the tabs and edges. Peel the backing from the tape on the base panel and place the box in position on the paper. Remove the tape backing on one side panel at a time; carefully fold the paper up and over the top edge, smoothing it down as you go. Fold the tabs over. Repeat with the remaining side panels.

2. Cover the inside of the box

Trace around the outside of the side panels and bottom of the box. The inside will be slightly smaller, so cut each piece 1 mm in from the traced line. Remember it's easy to cut more off, but you can't add it on again. So only cut 1 mm off at first. Test the paper inside the box. If it is too big, cut another 1 mm off. Once the four sides and base papers are the right size run some double-sided tape along the top and bottom edges of the box sides and peel off the backing one side at a time. Carefully stick the paper in. If you want to add more layers of papers or different papers to each section, now is the time.

3. Arrange display items

Lay out your display items. Consider their size, shape, colour and depth, then place them in the box. Move them around, add and subtract things until you are happy with the layout. Decide how to attach your items. Light items can be secured with double-sided tape and oddly shaped or heavy things may need sticky-backed Velcro dots.

4. Make supports

For objects to sit in the foreground and stay in place you'll need to add a strut behind them. A strut is like a mini shelf or bracket. To make it, fold a piece of cardboard into a rectangle that is small enough to be hidden by the object attached to it and tape it in place with some double-sided tape. Stick your item in front of it and hold it in place with tape or a sticky-backed Velcro dot. A card or photo can be stuck to a small lid or matchbox, which is then attached to the back wall of the box. Other items like small toys can be attached to a cardboard strut.

5. Add a frame

To make a framed shadow box, start with a box that has a separate lid like a gift box or shoebox. If you want to cover or decorate the lid, do that before you cut the frame shape out. Place the lid right side down on your cutting mat. Draw the frame shape onto the inside of the lid. Carefully cut around the shape using a craft knife on a cutting mat, then attach the lid in place, with double-sided tape.

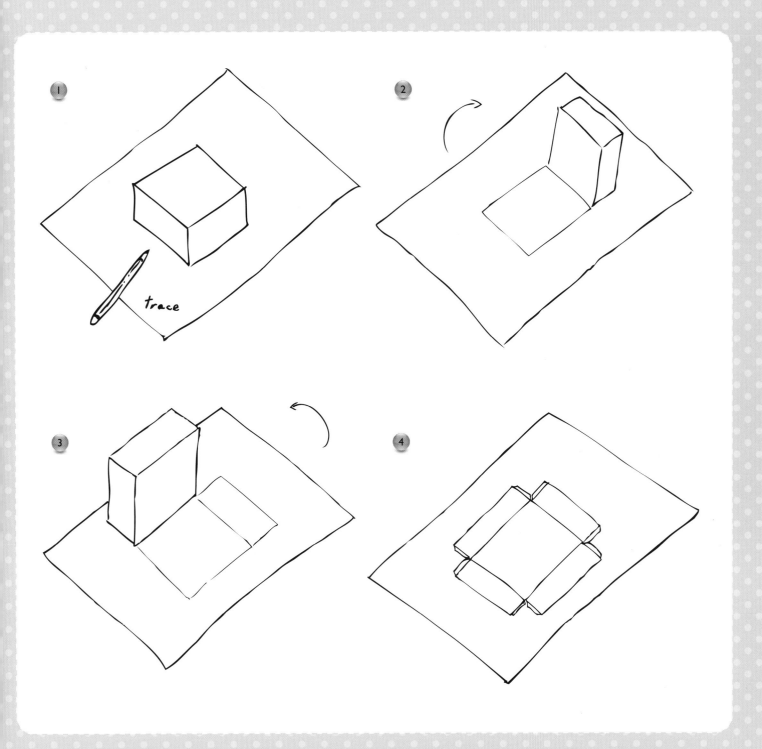

1

trace

2

3

4

spruce your space

Is your room your castle? Do you love nothing better than to close your door, put on some music and enjoy your privacy? With the projects in this section you will be able to make your room your own, decorate it to your liking and make it even more cool than ever before. If you like flowers there are two flower projects that you can make to attach to your walls. There are three projects you can make to hang from your ceiling or window, where they will flutter in the breeze and catch the light. Or why not make some origami light shades for a set of string lights — perfect for night-time!

Before getting started on these projects, get organised! Don't forget to clear your area first, gather your materials, read the chapters on safe handling of tools and equipment, and ask for help if you need it. For most of the projects in this section, you'll need just a few basic items to get started: paper, of course, glue, tape and scissors. There is one project that will require the use of a craft knife and another project for which a needle and thread will come in handy, but if you don't have these tools or haven't used them before, don't fret! Read the instructions and check with your parents first: you might need a little help to get started, but after that you should be fine on your own.

wallflowers

pretty rolled flowers

clouds and raindrops window hanging

kirigami snowflake and star

miniature mobile birds

origami cube lights

Wallflowers

Brighten any room or party with these colourful flowers made from paper napkins. They're easy to make and the options are endless! The paper napkins give the flowers a lovely structure – they almost look like fabric. They are very easy to make and add a lovely touch to any sort of celebration – use them on gifts or even for your day-to-day room decor.

project by: dana willard
suitable for: beginners
should take: less than 1 hour

SHOPPING LIST

- Good-quality 3-ply party napkins in several colours
- String, twine or twist ties

CRAFTY NEEDS

- Scissors

NOTES

- Tissue paper will also work but napkins make the flowers stiffer, so you can shape them better. Use a few different colours, stripes, or dots to create interesting combinations.
- To hang the flowers, attach them with string, tape, or wire twist ties to a piece of twine or rope, and hang them on a wall.

1. Prepare the napkins

Take four large napkins, unfold them, and lay them on top of each other in a stack. To make a contrasting centre to your flower, place one or two different-coloured napkins on top of the stack.

2. Fold the flowers

Fold your stack of napkins up like a fan, or an accordion, back and forth right to the end – make your folds about 2 cm wide.

3. Tie the centre

Pinch the centre of the flower together and use a piece of string or a wire twist tie to hold it together in the middle (see diagram 1).

4. Trim the petals

Using scissors, cut a semi-circle out of each end of the folded flower. (see diagram 2). To give your flowers a spiky look, cut the ends away in negative semi-circle shapes (see diagram 3).

5. Finishing

Carefully pull the flower open, making sure you don't rip the napkins. Pull the edge of each petal up and towards the centre and away from the other petals (see diagram 4). Use scissors to trim and tidy up any edges.

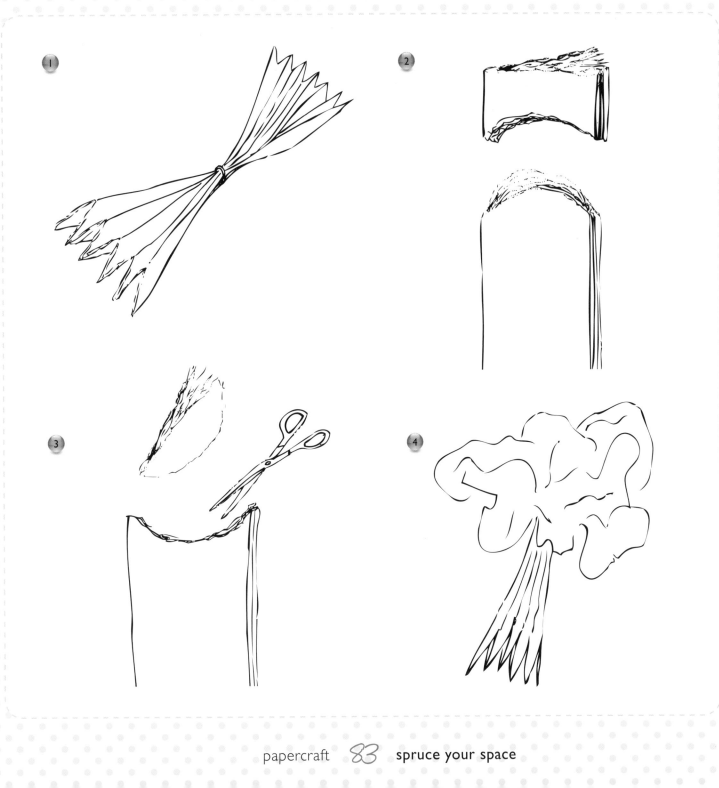

Pretty Rolled Flowers

Grow yourself an instant garden of fresh and fancy flowers. Make these paper blooms in different colours and patterns, and decorate them with anything you choose – from pompoms to beads and buttons. When you're finished you will have petals with pizzazz!

project by: olivia kanaley
suitable for: beginners
should take: about 1 hour

SHOPPING LIST

- Paper for flowers and leaves
- Decorations – such as mini pompoms, beads or buttons for centre of flower, and sewing trims for the edges of flower (optional)

CRAFTY NEEDS

- Pencil
- Scissors
- Quick-drying paper glue

NOTES

- If you are feeling confident, try adding trim to the edge of your flower. Before rolling up the flower in Step 4, glue sewing trim to the back of the paper along the scalloped edge. Be sure to use sewing trim: it has an extra allowance for easier gluing. This technique can also be used along the edges of the leaves.
- The centres of the flowers can be decorated with anything you like, such as pompoms, fancy buttons or pretty beads.

1. Draw the flower shape

On the back of a patterned or coloured piece of paper, draw a spiral shape. Now add a scalloped line along the spiral (see diagram 1). Cut out the shape by cutting only along the scalloped line, not your initial spiral line (see diagram 2). When you have finished cutting, lay the paper on the table face up.

2. Roll up the flower

Starting from the centre of the spiral, begin rolling the paper to form the flower (see diagram 3). The decorative side of the paper should face inward. When you have finished rolling, let the flower unroll naturally.

3. Make the flower base

Cut a circle from the same paper as your flower. It needs to be big enough to fit the base of the flower. Put it face up on the table and cover it generously with glue. Roll up the flower again, as in Step 2. Place the flower on top of the circle and hold it in place until dry. Cut notches into the outside of the circle and fold the notches up to enclose the outside of the flower (see diagram 4). Glue the notches down.

4. Finishing

When the glue is dry, add decorations like a bead or pompoms to the centre of the flower. Cut out some paper leaves and glue them to the bottom of the flower.

Clouds and Raindrops Window Hanging

Create some privacy, texture and colour in your room with this window hanging. Make one or two strings to hang in a corner of your room, or make 20 to hang over your door.

project by: khali whatley
suitable for: beginners
should take: about 2 hours, depending on how many you make

SHOPPING LIST

- Patterned and coloured paper
- Glue
- Lengths of coloured ribbon
- Blu-Tack

CRAFTY NEEDS

- Scissors

TEMPLATES

- You will need the Clouds and Raindrops Window Hanging template for this project, or you could make your own templates by drawing a simple design freehand.

NOTES

- Use Blu-Tack to secure the ends of the ribbon to a doorway, roof or wall. You could also tie them onto a length of dowel or a coathanger.
- Thick paper or card is best for this project. For the best effect, try limiting the number of shapes.

1. Cut out shapes

Trace your templates onto patterned and coloured paper. Use scissors to cut out a back and a front of each paper shape (see diagram 1). You will need about 15 circles, five clouds and five raindrops for every length of ribbon. If you have a large circle cutter (available from craft and scrapbooking shops) this will make this job a bit quicker.

2. Prepare the ribbon

Measure your door or window height and then cut lengths of ribbon to match. Place the shapes evenly along the length of the ribbon, alternating different shapes and colours. Arrange all your shapes before you begin gluing them onto the ribbon to make sure you will be happy with the end result.

3. Finishing

Glue the front and the back of each paper shape together with the ribbon secured in between (see diagram 2). Hang your clouds and raindrops against a window, door or wall (see diagram 3).

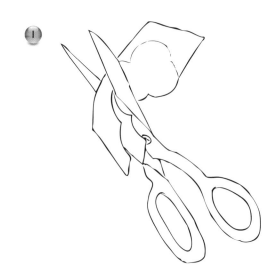

CRAFT GLUE

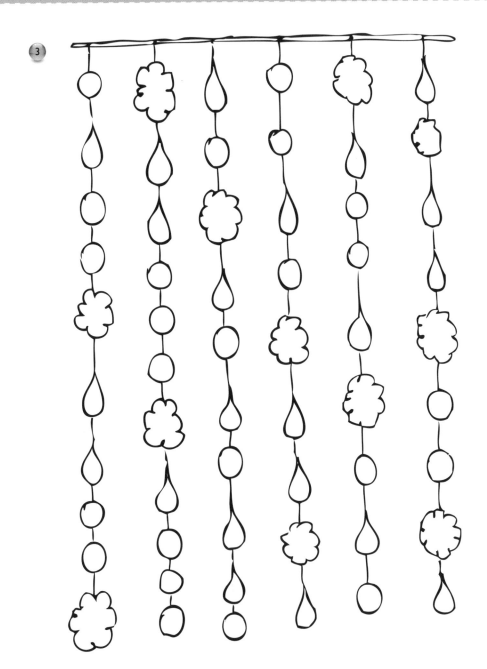

Kirigami Snowflake and Star

Kirigami is a Japanese paper-cutting technique that combines folding with paper-cutting to create a symmetrical pattern. This kirigami snowflake and star is a cut-and-fold project based on a combination of kirigami and origami techniques to make a seasonal card or a fun decoration.

project by: elod beregszaszi
suitable for: confident beginners
should take: 1–2 hours

SHOPPING LIST

• A5 size medium-weight coloured card stock (needs to be robust enough to stand up, but thin enough to fold easily)

CRAFTY NEEDS

• Scissors
• Pencil

TEMPLATES

• You will need to choose a Kirigami Snowflake and Star template for this project. There are two different snowflakes templates and one star template.

NOTES

• Don't worry if the project doesn't work the first time – just have another go. Paper is a relatively cheap material so you can practise as much as you like.
• In all origami projects, folds are described as either mountain or valley folds. A mountain fold comes out towards you (in the shape of a capital letter A in the cross-section) while a valley fold recedes away from you (in the shape of a capital letter V in the cross-section).

1. Prepare the template

Choose a template, then trace the template onto paper or cardboard and cut it out before starting.

2. Cut the shape

Place the template on top of your coloured card and align it as shown in the diagram on the template. Fold your card in half. Take your pencil and draw around the inside edge of your template (see diagram 1). Remove the template and cut along the drawn lines with your craft knife, through the two layers of card. Take care not to cut across the spaces between the cutting lines (see diagram 2).

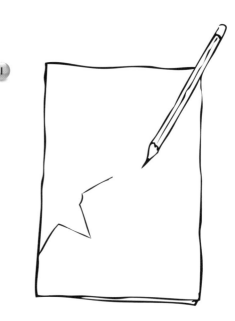

3. Unfold the card

Push the cut portion of the design out from left to right and press down firmly along the vertical line running down the centre. Then very carefully unfold your card. Take your time over this to avoid tearing.

4. Pop the shape out

To make your shape pop forward from the background, fold the vertical line (currently a valley fold) and change it into a mountain fold. To do this, gently pinch along the crease line from the top while pushing the shape out from below (see diagram 3). Slowly collapse the model, pinching the four corners of the star or snowflake into valley folds. Once flat, press down on the paper and go over the folds with your finger to strengthen the creases.

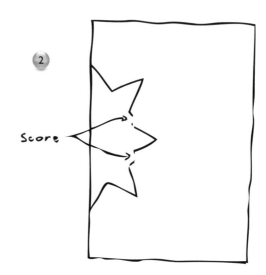

Score

5. To make a hanging decoration

With a small modification you can change this project from being a card into a hanging decoration for your window. Follow step 1, then at step 2 draw around both the inside and outside edges of the template (see diagram 4) and cut along both lines, being careful not to cut through the vertical marked line. Then continue to follow the remaining instructions as for the card above, taking extra care when popping your shape out from the background.

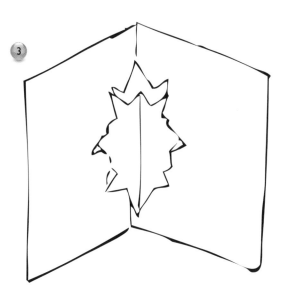

> #### Cutting with scissors instead of a knife
>
> *If you don't want to use a craft knife, you can make this project with scissors simply by making an extra fold in your original piece of card. Take your piece of A5 card and fold it in half from left to right, then fold in half again from top to bottom. Don't turn the card around – you should have the open sides on the bottom and right hand sides of your folded card. Place your template on top of your card and align the horizontal side to the top edge of the card, and the vertical side to the left edge of the card. Take your pencil and draw around the inside edge of your template, marking the small vertical line. Remove the template and use your scissors to cut along the drawn lines from two sides as shown. Take care not to cut across the space.*

Miniature Mobile Birds

These small and sweet paper birds are easy and fun to make. You will want to make a few in different papers and then hang them from your bedroom ceiling. Add some paper leaves and flowers, and use a rustic branch to bring the outside world into your room.

project by: erin hall
suitable for: beginners
should take: 2–3 hours

SHOPPING LIST

- Decorative heavy-weight paper for birds
- Coloured papers for flowers and leaves
- Embroidery thread or fishing line (for hanging birds)
- Ribbon (for hanging branch)
- Clear-drying craft glue
- Branch (for hanging birds from)
- Small eye screw (which you can find at the hardware store)

CRAFTY NEEDS

- Scissors
- Small hole puncher
- Craft knife
- Binder clips

TEMPLATES

- You will need the Miniature Mobile Birds template for this project.

NOTES

- Trace or photocopy the templates for the birds, flowers and leaves onto different heavy-weight paper or card stock. Paper can be patterned, coloured or plain.
- Find a small branch from your yard or nearby park, inspect it for bugs and clean off any leaves or loose bark before bringing it inside. You could also use bamboo sticks from a gardening store, a length of dowel from the hardware store, or even a wire coathanger. Birds can also be hung from houseplants, centrepieces or small hooks in the ceiling, instead of using them in a mobile.

1. Cut out the birds

Cut out the birds, wings, and tail-pieces on the solid lines. Punch a hole in the bird body using a small hole puncher where indicated by the dot. Using scissors, snip a small slot in the tail end of the bird for inserting the tail later. Cut along the wing line in the bird's body using a craft knife on a protected surface.

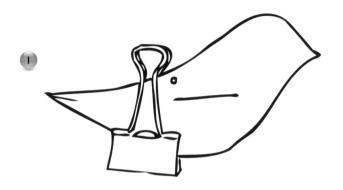

2. Add the wings

Secure a binder clip to the belly of the bird behind the wings so that it can stand up as you glue the wings in place (see diagram 1). Insert the wings into the wing slot and glue on the underside (see diagram 2). Insert the tail into the slot made earlier and secure with glue (see diagram 3). Stand to dry (drying time will depend on the type of glue you have used).

3. Make flowers and leaves

While the glue sets on the birds, cut out the templates for the flowers and leaves (see diagram 4). For some variety, glue some smaller flowers into the centre of the larger flowers and add small circles to the centre of some of the flowers. Cut these from coordinating papers using a hole puncher. Set these aside to dry: they will be used for decorating the branch later.

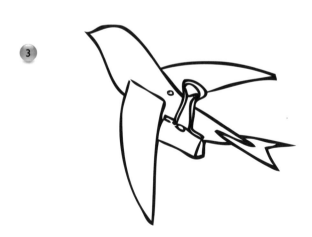

4. Tie on the string

Once the glue on your birds has dried, insert a strand of embroidery thread or fishing line into the hole on the bird's back and tie it in a knot. The line can be as long or short as you like, but 30–40 cm is good if it's going to be hung off a branch.

5. Attach to the branch

Take your branch and screw in the eye screw somewhere in the centre, so that when it hangs it will stay level. Tie on the birds at varying heights (see diagram 5), securing strings in place with a dab of glue. Then glue on flowers and leaves to add extra elements of colour. Once all the glue has set, hang your arrangement from a hook in the ceiling with decorative ribbon and enjoy it as it floats in the breeze.

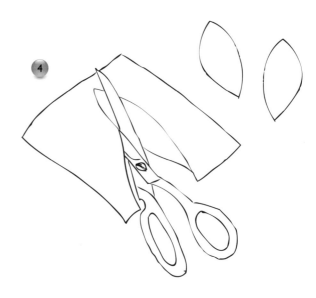

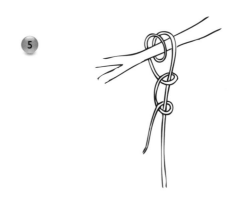

Origami Cube Lights

These light shades are so pretty and easy to make. By using different coloured papers, you can change the look and feel of your room. (As a bonus, you can make a few extra origami cubes and use them as water bombs!)

project by: rob shugg
suitable for: confident beginners
should take: 2–3 hours

SHOPPING LIST

- 20 cm squares of thin paper, such as rice paper, in different colours
- String of LED lights, approximately 12 lights
- Drinking straw

CRAFTY NEEDS

- Scissors

NOTES

- Rice paper is best for this project, because you want the light to shine through the paper.
- If you can get solar-powered LED lights, you can rest the solar power source on your windowsill so it powers up during the day and comes on automatically at night.
- This origami cube is also known as an origami water bomb: just fill with water and throw it straight away.

1. Prepare the paper square

Place your square paper on a flat surface with the coloured side down and fold on the diagonal. Unfold it and fold on the other diagonal, then unfold it again. Finally, fold it in half, then unfold it once more (see diagram 1).

2. Make a triangle

Fold the horizontal line up, and the corners on the right and left of the line behind it. The result will be two triangles lying on top of each other (see diagram 2).

3. Make a diamond

Place the resulting triangle with the point facing up. Fold the points of the bottom corners on the top side of the paper up to the top point. Then turn the paper over and do the same thing on the other side. This will result in a diamond shape (see diagram 3).

4. Tuck in the points

Fold the small corners of the diamond towards the centre. Do this on each side. Fold the small triangles at the base over the line that the last step's fold has made. Open the little pocket created, and slip the small triangles at the side into the pocket (see diagram 4).

5. Blow up the cube

Open up the side flaps of the paper shape. At the top there is a small hole: blow into the hole and the shape will expand to create a cube (see diagram 5).

6. Attach the cube to the light

Cut a drinking straw into 3 cm long pieces, then with small scissors, cut a cross shape into the top of the straw piece (see diagram 6) and bend it outwards (see diagram 7). Slip this into the hole at the top of the cube and place the other end of the straw onto the LED light (see diagram 8). This will hold the cube in place. Now make enough cubes for all of the lights and hang it up in your room.

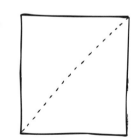
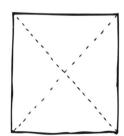
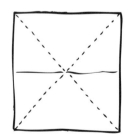
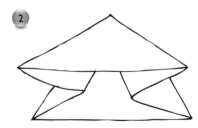

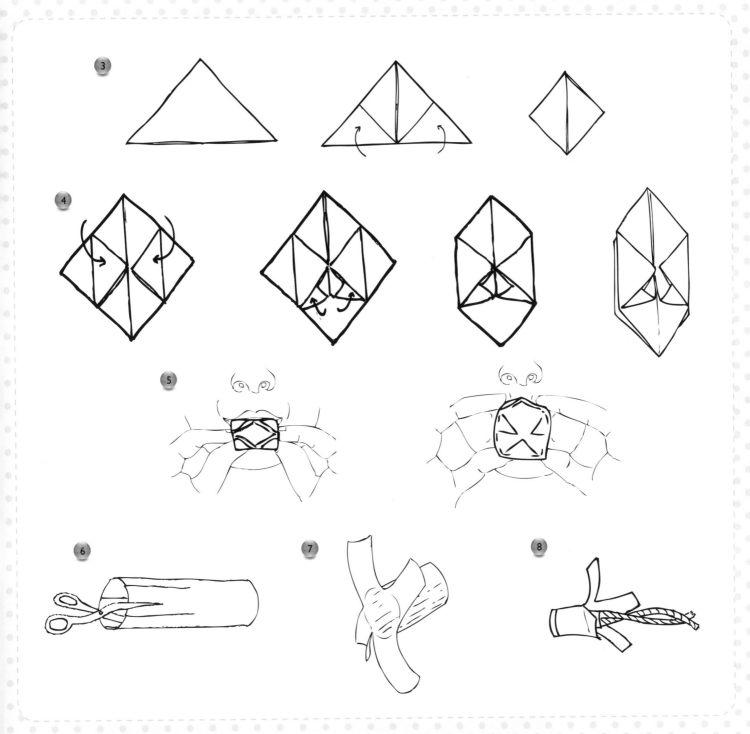

cute cards

Do you love to give presents just as much as receive them? *Mother's day, birthdays, Easter: do you spend hours making cards for your family and friends? You will love this chapter, which will give you some unique and fun cards to make for every occasion. If you want a quick project, you could make a sewn or pop-up card. If you love origami, put your skills to work. If you want a challenge, then make a cut-out house card or pop-up owl card that's almost too good to give away!*

Before getting started on these projects, don't forget to clear your area first, gather your tools and materials, and read the chapter on tool safety. Ask for help if you need it. Most of the projects in this section require just a few basic items to get started: paper, of course, glue, tape and scissors. There are a couple of projects requiring a craft knife, and another a sewing machine. If you don't have these tools or haven't used them before, don't fret! Read the instructions carefully and check with your parents first. You might need a little help to get started, but practice makes perfect so just give it a go.

Sewn Cards

Do you need a batch of cards in a hurry, but want something handmade, which looks impressive? Sewing on paper gives a polished finish and is really fast and effective.

project by: alison hudson
suitable for: beginners
should take: 1 hour

SHOPPING LIST

- Thin card (14.8 × 10.5 cm for each card)
- Decorative and recycled paper
- Glue stick

CRAFTY NEEDS

- Scissors
- Pencil
- A shape template, such as a cookie cutter
- Sewing machine and sewing thread or hand-sewing needle and thread

TECHNIQUES

- Hand sewing, page 12

TEMPLATES

- Make your template by using a cookie cutter or other shape (such as a star or cloud). Trace it onto cardboard and cut it out.

NOTES

- Use several layers of paper stacked together for a 3D effect when sewing your shape.
- Making cards is a great way to recycle paper – try using old comics, gift wrap, newspaper or magazines.
- This project uses a sewing machine but, if you don't have access to one, you can still make these cards by hand sewing instead. This will take a bit longer and you may need to pre-punch the sewing holes using a large embroidery needle, a nail or an awl.
- Use exactly the same technique to make a gift tag. Just stick the motif and background paper to a flat card or a luggage label.

1. Create the card

To create the base card, first take a sheet of thin card and fold it carefully in half, then set it aside for now.

2. Make a background

Cut out a piece of paper for your background, equal in size to the front of your base card, use a pencil and ruler to mark out a rectangle, using your base card as a guide. Cut it out with scissors.

3. Trace the template

Place your template onto your piece of decorative paper and trace around it (see diagram 1). If you want your card design to have several layers trace four or five of the same shape and cut them out (see diagram 2).

4. Position the shapes

Layer the shaped motifs in a stack (or your single motif, if you are only using one) and position it on the background paper that you cut out earlier. Using a sewing machine, sew a straight line of stitches through the centre of your shape and through all the layers, including the background paper (see diagram 3).

5. Glue the motif onto the card

Pull the thread, so the loose ends are on the back of the background paper and knot them together. Then use a glue stick to attach your background paper to the front of your base card. Take care to position it symmetrically and then leave it to dry under something heavy (such as a stack of books) to make sure it stays nice and flat.

6. Finishing

If you want your design to have a 3D effect: once the glue has dried, carefully pull each layer of the star upwards against the stitching line, so that the layers slightly fan out (see diagram 4).

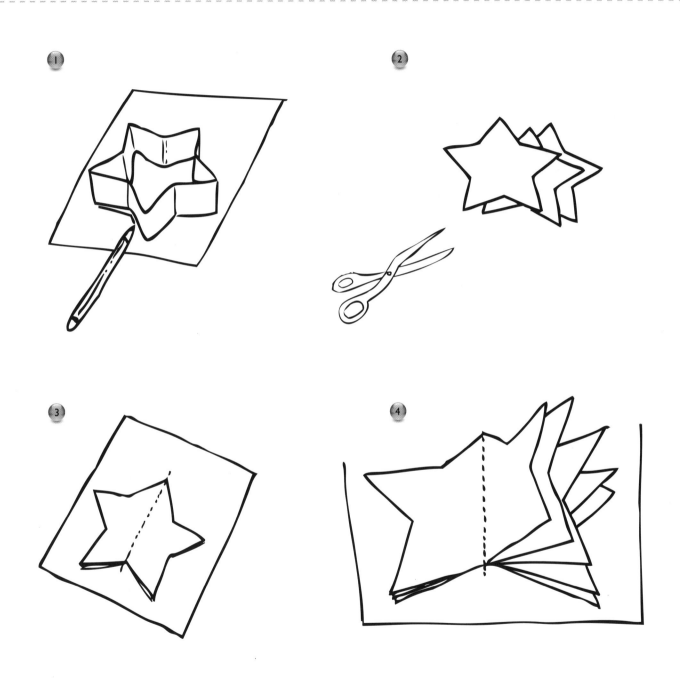

Pop-up Cards

Create a simple yet dynamic personalised card by using a photo and some pop-up magic!
Once you know how to make a pop-up hinge, you need never make a dull, flat card again.

project by: alison hudson
suitable for: beginners
should take: about 1 hour

SHOPPING LIST

- 2 pieces of thin A5 card
- Thin card in a contrasting colour
- Photograph
- Glue

CRAFTY NEEDS

- Scissors
- Pencil
- Ruler

NOTES

- You can decorate the front of the outer card any way you like. Marker pens, stickers or collage are all great ways to decorate – it is easier to do this when the outer card is flat, so get it ready before you glue your inner card into your outer card. Let your creativity run wild!
- When you are choosing a pop-up image, pick one about half the width of the folded card, so it fits neatly inside when the card is closed. If your photo is slightly bigger, you can shorten the length of your hinge to make it fit better. Experiment!
- Use this technique for any image you like: try cutting out images from magazines or old cards or even draw your own design!
- If you have a very tall picture, you might find that two hinges support it better. Follow the instructions, but make two hinges at the top and the bottom of the card and stick your picture to both of them.

1. Fold the inner and outer cards

Take two pieces of A5 card. One sheet is for the outer card, so fold it in half, decorate it if you like, and set it aside. The second sheet is for the inner card: first trim 1 mm off the top and from one side (use a ruler to draw a line first, then cut with scissors or a craft knife) so that it is a teeny bit smaller than the outer card. Fold the inner card in half.

2. Make the pop-up hinge

Take the folded inner card and draw two parallel lines, 3.5 cm long and 2 cm apart, from the folded edge on the outside of the card. The bottom line should be about 3 cm up from the bottom edge of the card. Cut along these lines with scissors, through both layers of the folded card, to make a tab (see diagram 1). Fold the tab forward, crease it firmly and then bend it back (see diagram 2). Now open the card and gently push the tab inwards so that it makes an elbow shape inside the card: this is your pop-up hinge (see diagram 3). Press the card firmly closed to make sure your hinge folds flat.

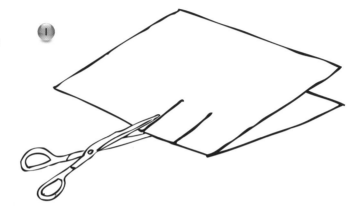

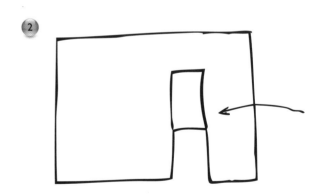

3. Design the pop-up

To prepare your pop-up design, first cut around the outline of your photograph and attach it with glue or double-sided tape to a piece of coloured card. It looks nice if this is in a contrasting colour to the one you picked for your inner card. If you want to include a speech bubble as part of your design, cut it from white card and attach it to the coloured card too. Then cut a single outline around both shapes, leaving a narrow margin of coloured card showing around the edge.

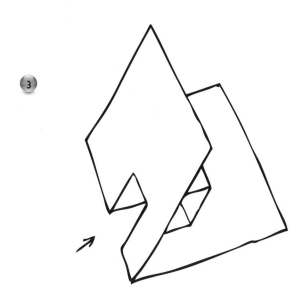

4. Glue the pop-up to the inner card

Make sure your pop-up will fit inside the card when it is glued to the hinge and the card is shut. If it pokes out when the card is shut, you may need to make the cuts for your hinge a little shorter, or use a narrower picture for your pop-up. Put a dab of glue on the front end of the hinge (see diagram 4) and attach the image to it. Be careful not to accidentally glue your card shut!

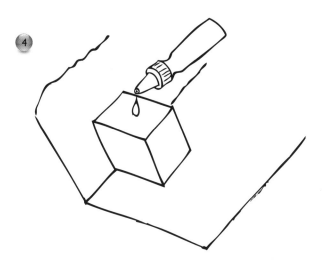

5. Glue the inner card to the outer card

Open up your outer card and spread glue all around the edges. Do not glue along the fold! Carefully position your inner card inside the outer card and leave it under a heavy object (such as a stack of books) to dry nice and flat.

Origami Cards

Here are two different origami card designs to make. One is a puppy-dog card that you can personalise with different facial expressions on the puppy. The other is a fashion card that's perfect to use as party or afternoon tea invitation.

project by: kathreen ricketson
suitable for: confident beginners
should take: about 2 hours

SHOPPING LIST

- Origami paper in different colours
  (12 cm squares for the bigger puppy
  and the fashion cards, or 5 cm squares
  for the mini puppies)
- Regular copy paper in different colours
  for the card
- Paper glue
- Red pencil or felt-tip marker
- Black felt-tip pen
- Glitter glue

CRAFTY NEEDS

- Scissors

NOTES

- Here are some ideas for messages to use
  on the puppy card: 'I wuf you', 'Be my best
  friend', 'Come wag a tail with me'.

WE

WUF

YOU

Cards

PUPPY CARD

Make the face

1. Take your square of origami paper and lay it with the coloured side down. Fold in half on the diagonal corner to corner (see diagram 1).

2. Fold the triangle in half again, then unfold (see diagram 2).

3. Place the triangle with the tip facing downwards. Fold the tip of the top layer of paper upwards by one-third, then fold the point of the tip down by half again (see diagram 3). This creates the puppy's nose.

4. Lift the top layer of paper up, to keep it out of the way, and fold the underside of the triangle tip. Fold the tip upwards by one-third, then fold the tip down by half again (see diagram 4). Fold the top layer of paper back down again.

Make the ears

5. Now create the ears, by folding down the top two corners of the triangle (see diagrams 5 and 6). You can adjust the ears to your liking – fold them back up a little to create perky ears, or fold one up and leave one down.

Finishing off

6. Finish off your puppy by trimming the corner tip off the tongue and rounding it out (see diagram 7), then colouring it in with your red pencil or marker. Draw in the eyes. Colour in the nose and create some freckles with your black felt-tip pen (see diagram 8).

Complete the card

7. Take an A4 coloured piece of copy paper and fold it in quarters. Place glue onto the back of your puppy and glue it onto the front of your folded card. Print or stamp your message.

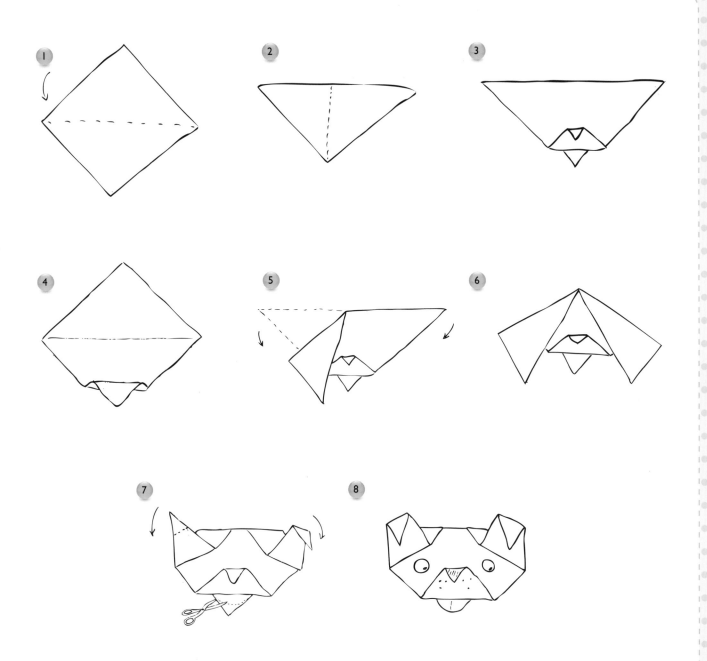

PARTY FROCK CARD

Make the dress

1. With the coloured side of the origami paper facing up, fold your paper in half, then in half again, then in half again, to make vertical creases (see diagram 1).

2. Pleat the two outer and the two inner folds towards the centre (see diagrams 2 and 3).

3. Fold the bottom up about 3 cm below the top, then back down again, to make the waistline of the dress (see diagram 4). Fold the two side pleats to the back and slightly open out the pleats of the skirt section (see diagram 5). Decorate with glitter glue and set aside.

Make the short jacket

4. With the coloured side of the paper facing down, fold your square of paper in half, then open it out and fold it in half again (see diagrams 6 and 7). Lay the paper flat again and fold the two outer edges into the centre (see diagram 8).

5. Fold the top of the folded paper down 2 cm (see diagram 9). Turn the paper over and fold in the sides on a slight angle (see diagram 10).

6. Open out the corners of the diagonal flaps and flatten them down to create the jacket collar (see diagram 11). Cut the jacket to the desired length (see diagram 12) and decorate with glitter glue if you like.

7. Slip the top part of the dress inside the jacket and glue it in place.

Complete the card

8. Take an A4 coloured piece of copy paper and fold it in quarters. Place glue onto the back of your party frock and glue it onto the front of your folded card. Print or stamp your message.

Home Sweet Home

It's so easy to make your own little house with doors and windows that open and close. Add window boxes that overflow with of flowers. Finish the scene with a little fence, since you don't want your bunny rabbits to escape! Perfect for small dolls to use as their home too. Give your 3D house card to your best friend or use it as an invitation to your next birthday party.

project by: cate holst
suitable for: confident beginners
should take: an afternoon

SHOPPING LIST

- White heavy-weight card stock
- Cardboard and papers in various colours
- 2 pieces of A4 striped paper for roof, doormat and flowers
- 6 brads
- Mini pompoms for bunny tails

CRAFTY NEEDS

- Scissors
- Glue stick
- Cutting knife, steel ruler and cutting mat
- Bone folder or butter knife, for scoring
- Push pin, tack or darning needle
- Sticky tape
- Paper edger scissors for scalloped edge along roofline (optional)
- Fine black marker

TEMPLATES

- You'll need the Home Sweet Home template for this project.

NOTES

- Trace or photocopy all templates. Roughly cut out the shapes 1 cm away from outer edges of traced templates and tape to cardboard or striped paper to secure
- The dotted lines on the template mean score and fold, not cut, while the solid lines mean you need to cut with a craft knife
- You can make your house using many alternative colour combinations. Add little fabric curtains in the windows, a tree for shade or a 'welcome' sign on the front door. Clouds or pompoms can emerge from the chimney instead of love hearts.

1. Cut out template shapes

Once your have taped the edges of your roughly cut out traced templates onto your white card, place this onto your cutting mat. First score along the dotted lines with your bone folder or butter knife and a ruler. Do this for the windows, door and centre slit. Then use a craft knife and ruler on your cutting mat to cut along the solid lines (see diagram 1).

2. Cut out decorative paper

Using scissors, cut out your house body side 1 and side 2. Then cut out four roof pieces and a doormat from your striped paper (optional: you can use fancy paper-edging scissors to cut the edges of the roof). Cut out your bunny rabbits, door, love hearts, flowers and wallhanging in various coloured cardboard or papers.

3. Assemble the house

Glue the roof front and back pieces to the top of each house. Cut a slit again on house side 1 using the traced template as a guide. Glue the door, doormat, wall hanging and heart-shaped cut-outs.

4. Add details

Gently prise open the cut-out window shutters and door so they hinge along the scored folds. Draw extra details onto the wooden window louvres, flower boxes, door knob, wall hanging and bunny rabbits with a fine black marker. Glue little pompom tails onto your bunnies' bodies, colour in their inner ears and insert their stands onto their bodies (see diagrams 2 and 3).

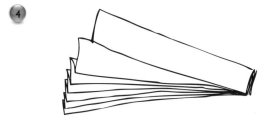

5. Make a garden

To help the flowers to stand up, use a push pin to create a hole in the flower and the place you want your flower to be positioned, then insert a brad and secure. Alternatively, simply glue the flowers onto the house.

6. Finishing

Gently slide the two house sides onto each other. Cut the slits slightly wider if they don't slide on easily

7. Fence

The fence is an optional extra. To make it, roughly measure a length of A4 paper and mark every 2 cm as a guide. Using a concertina fold (folds back on itself), make a fold every 2 cm (see diagram 4). Holding the folded paper in one hand, carefully cut out fence posts using the Fence template as a guide (see diagram 5). Unfold the fence (see diagram 6) and position it in front of the house.

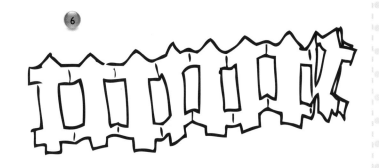

Owl Cards

You can have heaps of fun making these colourful 3D owl cards and adding your own personal message. There are shortcuts you can take if you're not confident in your papercraft skills.

project by: larissa holland
suitable for: confident beginners
should take: an afternoon

SHOPPING LIST

- 22 x 28 cm piece of card stock
- Scraps of card stock in various bright colours
- Ten 6 mm round pop dots
- Four 13 mm round pop dots

CRAFTY NEEDS

- Gel glue or glue stick
- 15 mm circle punch
- 25 mm circle punch
- Scissors
- Pencil
- Ruler
- Bone folder or butter knife for scoring
- Pinking shears, optional
- White gel pen for message

TEMPLATES

- You will need the Owl Cards template for this project.

NOTES

- If you don't have circle punches, use the circle templates as a guide to trace and cut your circle shapes from coloured card.
- Experiment with different colours or place the irises in different spots for different expressions.
- Shortcuts for an easier owl: skip the pinking shears steps; leave the beak flat, without the score and fold step; skip the pop dots; use small circles for the eyes, without eyelids; skip the ruff and wing accents.
- If you don't have pop dots, substitute small pieces of thick cardboard or foam sheets and use double-sided tape to attach them.
- Ideas for messages: 'Owl always love you'; 'Owl miss you'; 'You're a hoot'; 'Hooooo loves you? I do', 'Owl be seeing you'.

1. Cut out the pieces

Trace the template pieces onto coloured card stock. Use a pencil point to hold down the small pieces while tracing around them. Use the ruler and bone folder to score down the middle of the beak, then cut out all the pieces using scissors. If you have pinking shears, use these where noted. Add the slit in the wing. Mark the placement of the ruff on the front with pencil marks. Crease the beak along the score line.

2. Make the eyes

Use the 25 mm circle punch to punch two white circles for the eyes and one coloured circle for the eyelids (or you can skip the eyelids altogether). Cut the coloured circle in half to make two lids. Use the 15 mm punch to punch out two circles for the irises. Glue the irises onto the eyes, then glue on the eyelids. Place a 13 mm pop dot inside each circle on the face and put the eyes on top so they are centred (see diagram 1).

3. Add the ruff

Put a 6 mm pop dot in the centre of the back side of ruff A and B. Glue the top edge of ruff B aligned to the top edge of ruff C. Glue the top edge of ruff A aligned to B (see diagram 2). Then glue the assembled ruff onto the owl front, lining it up with your guide marks. When it is dry, flip it over and trim the overhang (see diagram 3).

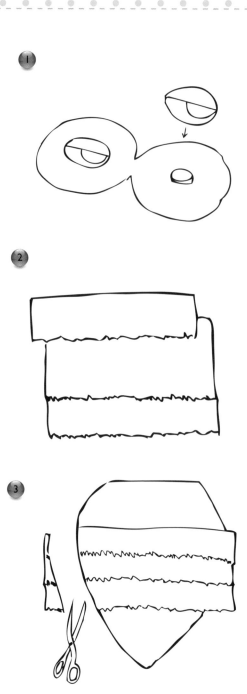

4. Put the owl together

Glue the assembled owl front onto the owl wings. Put two 13 mm pop dots onto the back of the face. Place the face onto the front with the straight part aligned with the top of the ruff. Place two 6 mm pop dots, stacked, in the crease on the back of the beak near its top and place it in the centre of the face. Place one 13 mm pop dot on the back of the brow, near the point, and place it between the eyes so that the point is touching the beak.

5. Add accents

Flip the owl over. Place a 6 mm pop dot near the bottom of both wing accents and then add glue to just the top corners. Place them so they are aligned with the shape of the wing (see diagram 4). Flip the owl back over. Punch four 15 mm circles for the toes. Put a 6 mm pop dot on the back of each toe, near its edge. Place these hanging halfway over the edge of the owl, below the ruff, in two groups of two.

6. Finishing

Fold a wing over and hold it in place with the bottom with your finger while you crease it down where it joins the body (see diagram 5). Repeat with the other wing. To close the wings for giving or mailing, tuck one wing inside the slit in the other wing. Open the wings and write your message in white gel pen on the ruff.

Published in 2011 by Hardie Grant Books

Hardie Grant Books (Australia)
85 High Street
Prahran, Victoria 3181
www.hardiegrant.com.au

Hardie Grant Books (UK)
Second Floor, North Suite
Dudley House
Southampton Street
London WC2E 7HF
www.hardiegrant.co.uk

National Library of Australia Cataloguing-in-Publication Data:
Title: Papercraft / edited by Kathreen Ricketson.
ISBN: 9781742700410 (hbk.)
Series: Kids' crafternoon.
Subjects: Paper work.
Other Authors/Contributors: Ricketson, Kathreen.
Dewey Number: 745.54

Publisher: Paul McNally
Project editor: Jane Winning
Design and art direction: Heather Menzies
Photography: Alicia Taylor
Styling: Rachel Vigor
Editing: Melody Lord
Colour reproduction by Splitting Image Colour Studio
Printed in China by 1010 Printing International Limited